THE
INESCAPABLE
GOD

ISBN: 978-0-578-96990-9

Front cover image by Author: J. Carlyle Gill.
Book design by Crystal Heidel.

First Printing Edition 2021.

For more information, contact the author at: jcarlylegillauthor@gmail.com

THE
INESCAPABLE
GOD

Eric,
I remember you
well. May this
inspire. Carlyle

THE REV.
J. CARLYLE GILL

Blessings,
Carlyle

Dedication

To **Mary Helms** who found her voice against all odds and who encouraged me to share my voice.

To **Carolyn Wzorek** who has listened to my voice, edited my voice, never failed to give honest and loving suggestions, and lived with me for twenty-six years.

To the **Rector and people of St. Peter's Episcopal Church** in Lewes, Delaware whose generosity of spirit participates in the One Spirit who inspires us all.

Acknowledgements

Pat Okoniewski lovingly went through sermon manuscripts cataloging them, organizing them and with our editor, Ellen Collins, has brought this book to fruition.

The people of St. Peter's Episcopal Church in Lewes, Delaware are wonderful sermon listeners and without them there would be no sermons and no book.

The Rev. Jeffrey Ross is one of the most generous Episcopal priests I know. He supports and encourages each of the clergy at St. Peter's.

Table of Contents

Foreward

IN MODERN PARLANCE, THE WORDS "PREACH" AND "SERMON" HAVE somehow landed in a moralism category. We hear people say, "I don't want to be preached at" or "I didn't ask for a sermon on that topic" and various other disparaging uses of those words.

Actually the verb "to preach" comes from the Greek "logidsomai" which means to "lay the word on." Or simply, "to word." A good way to understand this meaning is to think about how we were "worded" as children. For example, when a father says to his little girl, "You are my beautiful princess," she feels like a princess and actually believes she is a princess. This "wording" will stay with her for a lifetime. Similarly, when a parent says to a child, "You're too fat," that child will wrestle with his or her body image for a lifetime.

The theological purpose of preaching is to lay on the Word of God, the "gospel," the Good News. I believe the Word laid on us is the same as that laid on Jesus: "You are my Beloved. With you I am well pleased." These are the words I have heard and I hope you hear them in my preaching.

— J. Carlyle Gill
All Saints Day 2021

Introduction

As a young teenager, I heard my mother ask my father one night at dinner, "Do you think you'll go to heaven?" He answered, without pausing for thought, "I think if you want to go there, you will." I wondered if it could be that simple. In my mother's voice I heard the fear that salvation was something that was not guaranteed, something held out by a capricious God. In my father's response I heard faith.

That was many decades ago. Reading Mother Carlyle's sermons as her editor, I have come to understand what my father meant. In these texts, I have discovered the God who welcomes all, embraces all, waits without judgment and rejoices with us, no matter our standing or situation. I have discovered the God who seeks the lonely, the downtrodden, the misunderstood.

The sermons in this book are arranged in four categories: Called, Awakened, Welcomed, and Transformed, signposts of our spiritual journeys. They are all infused with Mother Carlyle's view that preaching is about "laying on the word" from the Greek *logizomai*. That the Word laid on us is the same as that laid on Jesus: You are my Beloved. With you I am well pleased.

May you find in this book what it means to seek and to be sought and, most of all, to know yourself as beloved.

Ellen Collins

Called

There are many calls, and many ways to answer. We are called to relationship, to community, to ministry. On our physical and spiritual journey, we are called to listen, to witness, to reflect, to make choices and take chances.

What Does God's Call Mean to Us?

Then Jesus came from Galilee to John at the
Jordan, to be baptized by him.
Matthew 3:13

Etched on the cornerstone of the Bishop Payne Library at the Virginia Seminary are these words: "Seek the truth, cost what it will, come what may." I believe that came from the lips of Phillips Brooks, famous Episcopal preacher. Those words floated to me in the early morning as I was waking and worrying about this homily. I had been brooding, ruminating, pondering the meaning of call—God's call to us—since the Epiphany gospels are full of stories about call, as is the one this morning. Jesus says to those ordinary working-class guys who have spent their lives fishing, "Come, follow me." And they do it.

Hebrew scripture likewise abounds in call stories from Moses onward. Moses is doing his ordinary day job—tending the flocks of his father-in-law—when God interrupts in the form of an angel and as a bush on fire. Moses hears his name and a job description—to lead his people from bondage in Egypt to a promised land. "No, not doing it," Moses replies. "I don't speak well enough, and no one will listen to me. Try my brother." But God persists, and Moses signs on. It's not a pretty story from then on. At one point in that arduous journey from bondage to freedom, Moses laments, "Why did you lead me out here in the middle of nowhere with all these pesky people who can only complain?"

Jeremiah also senses that his call is for a job too big for him. At one point, having really upset the dominant order—the Judean kings—Jeremiah says to God, "I quit. I've had it. I'm done." But, after thinking about it for a while, he explains, "Even if I said I wouldn't speak in your name, I cannot *not* because it is like a fire pent up in my bones, and I am weary from holding it in" (Jeremiah, 20:9).

So just from these two Hebrew prophets, my musings about call began to change from some light and almost poetic thoughts to the truth of call, that it is weighty, dangerous, and costly. Moses never gets into the promised land. He dies at its edge. Jeremiah is tortured in unspeakable ways. And the cross of Christ is the central image of our faith.

So, what does call mean for us, you and me, today, now, in our lives? I believe there is as much urgency to the work of God in our world as there was for the prophets in theirs. God's call is to all of us for the sake of our world and our country. First, we need to be open to seeing what is happening. It's so easy, so much more comfortable, to live in denial. But if we do, hatred will flourish. Did you know that there are groups of people who were prepared to go to the Richmond, Virginia gun festival and urge people to do harm to synagogues and black churches? Will the fundamentals of our government, our way of life, survive? Given the realities of climate change, will this fragile earth, our island home, survive?

I ask, seeking the truth no matter its cost, how are we called? Given these issues, to what are we called? What would God have us do now? We, too, are ordinary people living our ordinary lives, tending our flocks, fishing, keeping body and soul together. How, then, might God be calling us?

I actually think the answers to my questions are not in the *back* of the book, but in the *middle* of the book, *The Book of Common Prayer* (p. 302, 305), in the baptism service. Two of the baptismal questions are:

Do you renounce Satan and all the spiritual forces of wickedness that rebel against God?

Do you renounce the evil powers of this world which corrupt and destroy the creatures of God?

And two of the baptismal covenant questions are:

Will you seek and serve Christ in all persons, loving your neighbor as yourself?

Will you strive for justice and peace among all people and respect the dignity of every human being?

If we lived into our baptism, our call to be and to act as the people of God, the body of Christ, wouldn't that be enough? What if I, for example, asked myself those questions every day? Lived those questions every day? Wouldn't that be enough?

Yet even if we answer and live those questions every day, we may, like Moses, find ourselves in the wilderness wondering why on earth we ever agreed to this. Or we may be tempted like Jeremiah to quit, to give up because it's too hard.

Or, we may live in the reality of Christ crucified as Paul tells the church at Corinth. I'm not sure what that means, but I think the reality of Christ crucified acknowledges, even given the evil powers of this world, that God's love for this world remains in weakness. I don't know. I've raised more questions than I can ever answer for myself or for you, but for now, I'm sticking to Phillips Brooks' quote on the Virginia Theological Seminary wall. "Seek the truth, cost what it will, come what may."

The Issue with Following

*Be on your guard against all
kinds of greed; for one's life does
not consist in the abundance of
possessions.*
Luke 12:15

FOR AT LEAST THE LAST MONTH WE HAVE BEEN HEARING GOSPEL
stories about what it means to follow Jesus. What it means to
walk the talk. What it means to be a disciple, to have a spiritual
discipline, to practice it. It's not about what we know. It's about
what we do. How we follow. And that's not so easy.

I think the late Verna Dozier, theologian and teacher, was
right on when she said, "Jesus does not ask us to believe in him.
He asks us to follow him." For at least the last month Jesus has
told us stories about following. Luke, the organizer of these stories, begins by saying, "Jesus set his face toward Jerusalem" (Luke
9:15). What a great sentence! Jesus didn't turn left onto Route One
but "set his face toward Jerusalem." A group gathers and follows
Jesus. Along the way questions are asked and stories told about
what it means to follow.

One of the first comes from a smart lawyer who wants to know what he must do to inherit eternal life. Jesus replies with a summary of the law. "You shall love the Lord your God with all your heart, mind, and strength, and love your neighbor as yourself," which the lawyer clearly should know (Mark 12:29-31). But trying to gain the upper hand, he asks, "Who is my neighbor?" This question is the occasion for a story about the good Samaritan. The answer embedded in the story is that the neighbor is the one who *does* something, who walks the talk, who takes the person from the ditch and cares *for* that person. The neighbor, the lawyer discovers, is the one who shows mercy, who *acts* mercifully. Like the tune from the Broadway show, *My Fair Lady*, "Don't Talk of Love, Show Me," or the Nike ad, "Just Do It."

In another example, those following along with Jesus ask about prayer. "Teach us to pray," they say (Luke 11:1). The story Jesus tells about prayer is action-packed. Prayer is about being in a living, active relationship with God, about engaging God. "Ask and it shall be given to you, search and you will find, knock and the door will be opened," Jesus says (Luke 11:9).

In other words, God is found in our asking, searching, knocking. This story reminds me of Blaise Pascal's conversion. Pascal was a brilliant mathematician and philosopher who searched for years for the presence of God. After years of searching, he heard God say, "Thou would not have searched for me had thou not already found me." The God we seek has already found us. Or as St. Augustine of Hippo once said, "God is closer to me than

I am to myself." And as Franciscan Richard Rohr says, we can't see what we are looking for at first because what we are looking for is also searching for us.

Today's gospel story about following is just a little more difficult, especially for us 21st century Americans. Someone asks Jesus to tell his brother to give him his share of the inheritance. Jesus begins this story by saying, "Be on your guard against all kinds of greed." And then he tells the story about the farmer who produced a bumper crop and is trying to figure out how to store such abundance, how to keep it for a day when, perhaps, there is a famine. A bigger barn, he thinks. That's what I'll do. Then I can relax, eat, drink, and be merry. This one is hard for us. Isn't more better? Shouldn't we be prepared for a rainy day? Shouldn't hard work pay off? Isn't it important to be secure?

Well, if I'd been on that dusty road to Jerusalem and heard that story, I'd be troubled. Really? What about my pension? Our house on the beach? Not to mention the iPad, iPhone, and all the other gadgets.

I think Jesus might reply something like this: "It's not about your stuff, Carlyle, your pension, your house on the beach, and all the rest. But it's about your attachment to those things, about what, who is most important to you." Hm-m-m, I would think about that.

Yes, attachment is the issue. Attachment is the energy of greed, attachment not only to our stuff but to our ideas, our feelings, our views of others, our views of how life should be. Attachment to our view of ourselves and our view of God. This might be the core issue in following, in discipleship, in spiritual practice. Our attachments keep us bound, stuck, imprisoned, unable to follow, to walk the talk. Attachment, whether to our stuff or our views, keeps us from truly seeing our neighbor in the ditch or anywhere else for that matter, and it keeps us from knowing the God who searches for us.

Perhaps letting go of our attachments, to our deeply held views, is *the* spiritual practice and the most difficult. After all, signing up for discipleship means setting our faces, with Jesus, toward Jerusalem, toward death. It might not be our physical death. It may in fact be harder. Setting our faces toward Jerusalem may mean dying to our attachments, to what we think is important but actually isn't.

The good news is that we are not on the road to Jerusalem alone, and our resurrection, our new life, happens in the letting go, so we are free to follow.

What's Love Got to Do with It?

*"Teacher, which commandment in the
law is the greatest?" He said to him,
"You shall love the Lord your God with
all your heart, and with all your soul,
and with all your mind. This is the
greatest and first commandment. And
a second is like it: "You shall love your
neighbor as yourself."*
Matthew 22:36-39

WE ALL HAVE QUESTIONS. WE ALL LIKE ANSWERS. MOST OF US don't like being left in the dark, not knowing something. Look at Adam and Eve. They couldn't stand the fact that God knew something they didn't. How come they didn't have access to the tree of the knowledge of good and evil? Why couldn't they have certainty? Get that apple, Adam!

We want to know. We believe we have the right to know. Almost every institution in our society is based on knowing or dispensing information. The news media feeds on our insatiable need to know. We have come to expect that our educational institutions will fill our bottomless need-to-know pits. Growing churches feed people answers, certainty, security. God can be known. Correct behavior can be known. Good and evil can be known. Good and evil people can be known.

So, you can't blame the Pharisees for wanting to know. After all, they had a lot to learn, a lot to know. There were 613 commandments and they tried earnestly to follow them all. Who can blame them for wanting to know a shortcut? Could there be just one? Could they follow the one and be holy instead of working so hard with the 613?

Jesus obliges with what we know as the summary of the law. Love the Lord your God with all your heart, mind, and soul. And love your neighbor as yourself. And there you have it! Two commandments rolled into one. Two instead of 613! The answer. Certainty. Love God. Love neighbor. Love self. Simple, huh?

Of course not.

Jesus' summary has its own complications in our culture because we have been trained to understand, to recognize, to know love as a feeling. What if I don't feel love for God? Others? Myself? How can I love if I've lost that lovin' feeling? I mean, think of this in terms of God. How do I love someone I've never seen? How do I love someone I can't understand? How do I love someone who is supposed to be in charge and yet can't seem to get things right anywhere in the world? Not to mention my own life. There is much biblical precedent for this conversation. The prophet Jeremiah said in a fit of pique, "I'm done. I've had it. I quit. Goodbye!"

If love is not a feeling, what is it? Jesus answered that question with stories, action stories. If there is someone left by the side of the road in a ditch, do something. Don't pass by. Jesus answered that question in the line of biblical prophets like Micah. "What doth the Lord require of thee but to love justice, do mercy, and walk humbly with thy God" (Micah 6:8). Love. Do. Walk.

Now, I'm going to take a different tack on the subject of love. Often, poets have wisdom about the nature of love. In her poem, "At the River Clarion," Mary Oliver describes sitting on a stone in the river, listening to the sounds of the water. And it comes to her that the water and the stone, and even the mosses under the water are speaking. And their message to her is that they are all part of a holy entity.

Perhaps love is learning to listen to mystery. Perhaps perceiving the mystery infused in this world is a way to the art of knowing and loving God. Learning to listen to mystery. This may be the task, the work of love.

But over time, seminaries have become dispensaries, sources of information, and answer providers. Answer providers, but not places where we can be initiated into mystery, into a reality that cannot simply be learned but must be experienced.

I think the same can be said of the church. While we come with questions, important questions, and would love to have the answers if not *the* answer, the really important questions in life elude simplistic answers. The church, too, is not a dispensary, but a place where we just might experience a baptism into mystery. Because when you think about it, really think about it, God is a mystery, and you and I are mysteries. What if we approached God as a mystery rather than a problem to be solved? What if we approached ourselves as an unfolding mystery? What if we saw others as mystery rather than beings to be manipulated, cajoled into doing what we want, or being who we think they should be?

These are important questions to ponder.

Smuggling God into the World

*And Mary said, "My soul magnifies the
Lord, and my spirit rejoices in God my
Savior, for he has looked with favor on the
lowliness of his servant. Surely, from now
on all generations will call me blessed."*
Luke 1:46-48

IT SEEMS TO ME THAT OVER THE YEARS I HAVE PREACHED MANY,
many times on the fourth Sunday in Advent—Mary's Sunday. I
wonder why that is. Is it because the designer of the rota thinks a
woman is better suited to preach about Mary? Is it just the luck of
the Rota Draw? Is it the Spirit at work? Perhaps the angel Gabriel
is behind it all, hoping that I will hear the message of the angels.
Whatever—it is Mary's Sunday. And I'm glad I'm the preacher
because I want not only to know more about Mary, I want to *be*
Mary. The real Mary. Not the Mary that has been handed to us by
countless church officials over the years. Not the Mary known as
meek and mild. Not the lady-like Mary. Not the Mary that most
of us of a certain age were asked overtly or covertly to emulate.
No. I don't want to be that Mary.

Because you see, Mary was an incredible person. For starters, she said "Yes" to the angel's bidding. An immediate yes. Not, "Well, I'll get back to you on that." But, "Yes! Yes! Be it unto me. Let's get on with it! I'm all in!" Actually, Mary is the first among those called who does that. You remember Moses said to Yahweh, "I don't think so. Not a public speaker. Try my brother." Or Isaiah who said, "Actually, I'm not such a good guy. You might want a really squeaky-clean person for the job. It's not me." But Mary, Mary says, "Yes." Yes. What an important word "yes" is. "Yes, I will marry you." "Yes, I love you." "Yes, I will go to seminary." "Yes, I will put one foot in front of the other no matter how hard it may be."

But Mary says more than yes. Mary is a prophet in the truest biblical sense. She is a *nabi* in the Hebrew: one who speaks for another. She speaks God's words. You can always tell when God is speaking because the lowly are lifted up. The hungry have good things. The rich have been sent away empty. This is the biblical God, the one we say has a preference for the poor, no matter in what form poverty comes. Poor living situation. Poor health. Poor in love. Poor in spirit. Poverty, no matter its source or kind, puts us in touch with our essential human nature: our vulnerability. Poverty, no matter its source or kind, disabuses us of the notion that we are God and allows us to be open to the real God. You can hear Mary the prophet speaking for God because she is speaking to the poor—all of us.

Mary's prophetic words are sung. Her song is commonly

called The Magnificat. Mary sings. This is not a theological tome or an exercise in systematic theology. Ask anyone in a choir what a difference singing makes. In order to sing, one uses almost every faculty a human being possesses—voice, energy, body, attention, soul, passion. Ask anyone in a choir and they will tell you that yes, you can sing alone, but it's much better to sing in a group. It's exponentially better. A choir becomes a body, a voice all its own.

Mary's words are a song. Meant to be sung by all of us, the choir known as church. Meant to embody all those qualities of singing. Her song begins with an exclamation: "My soul magnifies the Lord." In other words, my soul makes God big. Think of it. Think of those people whose souls make God big in your life. When we're around Mary's people, we get some sense of God's bigness, God's presence. Mary sings.

Mary is also what the Eastern Orthodox Christians call *Theotokos*—God-bearer. Medieval mystic Meister Eckhart described it eloquently.

We are all meant to be mothers of God. What good is it to me if this eternal birth of the divine Son takes place unceasingly but does not take place within myself? What good is it to me if Mary is full of grace, but I am not also full of grace? What good is it to me if this eternal birth of the divine son takes place unceasingly but does not take place within myself?

And Barbara Brown Taylor, contemporary theologian and preacher, translates theotokos this way (*Gospel Medicine*, p. 153):

You can take part in a thrilling and dangerous scheme with no script and no guarantees. You can agree to smuggle God into the world inside your own body.

Isn't that a wonderful translation of the word? To smuggle God into the world inside your own body? Mary is prophet, singer, and God-bearer.

These dark days of Advent need Mary. Especially when fear and hatred are all around, when civility is decried as political correctness, when hatred of the "other" is rampant and encouraged. In these dark days of Advent, our Advent, we need prophetic voices, we need people able and willing to sing God's song, willing to make God big. And we need people willing to smuggle God into the world inside their own bodies. This Advent I pray for the grace to be the real Mary. And what does this look like?

In these dark times, I believe it means not giving into the ugliness of our world, not remaining silent but speaking up and out. Speaking, singing, from a place in ourselves that is awake, clear, and God-centered. How could carpet-bombing whole parts of the Middle East possibly be a stanza in God's song?

In these dark times, how do we help the poor no matter who they are or where they are, be they our neighbors, fellow parishioners, or refugees from war-torn homelands? How do we reach out and act so that those who are near to us or far away know they are cared for? How can some litmus test of who is deserving of our help possibly be a stanza in God's song? Being the real Mary is actually claiming and living our baptismal covenant, our commitment to action for God's sake. It is seeking and serving Christ in all persons, loving our neighbors as ourselves.

So the remaining and abiding Advent question—actually Mary's question to each of us—is where in our lives will we say YES, where will be the YES? Where will we be willing to risk our souls and bodies to be God-bearers, wherever we are?

May each of us be given the grace to hear the angel's greeting, "The Lord be with you. Do not be afraid."

Spiritual Practices

Series on Coping with COVID-19

A SONG HAS BEEN GOING THROUGH MY HEAD FOR ABOUT A WEEK. I think it comes from watching a HULU show, "Mrs. America," set in the early 70s. The song comes from the mid-60s, with the lyrics, "What the world needs now is love, sweet love." As songs often do, this one lodges in my brain and I find myself singing it either aloud or in my head. I think it is spot-on for our time. The song brings me to the topic of spiritual practice, because love is a spiritual practice, if not *the* spiritual practice.

What the world needs now *is* love, love in so many ways. Love of ourselves, our neighbors, and of the living God. As I watch the news, my heart goes out to the many, many people who have lost their jobs and are struggling to feed their families. People who have never had to do this are forced to go to food banks. And I worry about opening the country too soon, that action making more people sick. I believe that love requires that we care for each other in these times, providing whatever is needed and taking care that this pandemic does not get worse. The words of the prophet Micah come to mind. "He has told you, O mortal, what is good; and what does the LORD require of you but to do justice, and to love kindness, and to walk humbly with your God?" (Micah 6:8).

A week ago, the Stephen ministers had a conversation about grief during these times. It was, I thought, a great conversation because it is so important to give voice to how we really feel, what we miss, what we have lost, and that for which we grieve. In these conversations are the seeds of compassion and love, for ourselves, for our friends, and for those we don't know. If nothing else, this time is teaching us collectively some wonderful things—what really matters, how to share, how to care. I see spiritual practice not as a cure, or even as a "how" to get through these times, but as a way of *being* in any time. It is a way to cultivate wisdom, to deepen our ability to love.

So, I want to begin with Jesus, always a good place to start. One time, Jesus had a conversation with a lawyer who asked what he must do to inherit eternal life. Or, in other words, what he had to do to be fully alive. As fourth century bishop, Irenaeus, said, "The glory of God is humanity fully alive." Jesus answered the lawyer by saying, "Love the lord your God with all your heart, mind, and soul, and love your neighbor as yourself" (Mark 12:29-31). Jesus might have concluded, "And there you have it!"

We need first to acknowledge how difficult this time is, how dark our emotions can be, how unacceptable this time can seem.

So, the first practice I want to share is one I would call Accept and Embrace. In Buddhist nun and teacher Pema Chödron's wonderful book, *When Things Fall Apart*, she says that falling apart is both testing and healing. She explains that nothing really gets solved, but that things come together and fall apart again. This happens over and over. She proposes that healing is in the process of making room for it all, for the grief and the relief, the misery and the joy.

It is important to develop the capacity to hold all of this, to hold the grief, the relief, the misery, and the joy. A seminary professor of mine once said that the more we have to hold, whether it be grief, sadness, difficulty, or joy, the more spirit we need to help us in the holding. I think we can see this in Jesus' own life.

Life is a great teacher. Each of us is old enough to have endured much, and each of us has learned by now that some of the hardest experiences have been the best teachers. I tell people that having breast cancer was one of my best teachers and among the most powerful spiritual awakenings in my life. Another seminary professor of mind whose son committed suicide said, "I have been to the bottom, and it holds."

There are three practices that help me accept and embrace. One, of course, is a long, developed, multifaceted, practiced faith. I turn to scripture, to stories to help me, and especially to the psalms. And by faith I don't mean a simple, literal, and linear something, but a seasoned relationship that has ups and downs, that grows and changes. This relationship with God is, for me, the backdrop, the background of all my practices. It is as the theologian Paul Tillich said, "the ground of my being."

The other practice that helps me accept and embrace comes from my practice of Centering Prayer and my practice of Buddhist meditation. I would call it a "witnessing," or Accept and Embrace practice. We can, when we are still enough, listen, see, and deeply feel as a witness. For example, when I notice that I am sad, I can say to myself, "This is what sadness feels like." Or when I am angry, I can say, "This is what anger feels like." I become a witness, and in the process can see as well as accept and embrace.

Recently, I have discovered another memorable aspect of Accept and Embrace called Pet the Lizard. Dr. Rick Hanson, who is a psychologist with a special interest in neurobiology, writes a regular blog piece about practice called "Just One Thing." I have found his articles very helpful. Pet the Lizard, in essence, talks about dealing with fear, a primal emotion in our early, reptilian brains, and one many of us are facing now as the unknowns about Covid-19 grow. Hanson says when he was little, he was afraid of lizards, but he learned by petting them that little by little his fears decreased. He recommends that when we are afraid, we remember that we are well, safe, and protected so that those feelings become stronger than our fears. He talks about the neuroplasticity of the brain, which means how the brain can be trained to calm the reptilian brain that has a fight or flight response to threats. As Hanson says, "your inner iguana needs a lot of petting." Or, in other words, a lot of awareness of safety, protection, and wellness. He recommends that we soothe our bodies, take deep breaths, shift to a comfortable position, and cultivate an awareness that we are safe, that necessary things are being accomplished, that we are doing fine and are alive and well.

Accept and Embrace is a way of loving and a way of becoming fully alive, because the only way we can truly accept and embrace ourselves and others is by *loving* ourselves and others and by receiving the unconditional love that God has for us. Gospel story after gospel story is about this action of God's unconditional love for us. The gospel story that converted me is the story of the woman who crashed Simon the Pharisee's dinner party. Jesus loved her just as she was, and I learned that I was loved just as I was. The fact that many in our parish are talking together about difficult emotions and difficult situations is a sign of love for each other. We are already engaging in this practice of accept and embrace.

The second spiritual practice I would simply call Paying Attention. It's among my favorites. Presbyterian minister and theologian Frederick Buechner wrote a wonderful story called "The Innkeeper." In it, he presents the character of the innkeeper who said "No Room." The innkeeper tells us how hard it is to run an inn, that it's like being lost in a forest of a million trees and every tree is something to be done. At the end of the story he says, "What am I to tell you? When the baby came, when nobody turns into somebody.....When the baby came, I missed him. All your life long you wait for your own true love to come, and when he came, I missed him."

It's a sad and true story at a deep level about our inability to pay attention. Simone Weil, a spiritual writer, once said, "Prayer is paying attention." Poets are especially good at that. Mary Oliver describes how her purpose in walking is to notice what is around her, the little things one might easily overlook. A stone, a weed. Praying, she writes, is "the doorway into thanks."

Anglican Benedictine and writer Esther de Waal once said that she carried a magnifying glass with her on her walks so that she could see, could pay close attention.

Annie Dillard wrote a wonderful book, *Pilgrim at Tinker Creek*. In it, she talks about seeing, about paying attention. She tells a story from her childhood when she would plant pennies along the sidewalk in front of her house. She would then draw chalk arrows and the words, "Surprise ahead! Money this way!" Then she would watch to see who excitedly discovered the pennies she had planted. She reflects that the world is planted in pennies waiting for us to uncover them.

On a retreat in the high desert of southern California I developed my own paying attention spiritual practice. I called it Padding. It is very simple. Essentially, you walk very slowly, noticing as much as you can, attending, allowing yourself to be surprised by what you see. You take nothing for granted. The only rule is to never, never, be in a hurry.

The third practice I call Simply Being, and it may be the

hardest of all. We are so used to doing, to performing, to achieving, that simply being can be well-nigh impossible. For me, Simply Being takes many forms. It can be a slow, meditative walk where I pay close attention to my steps, to how it feels to walk, to what is in my path. Often at the Buddhist sangha retreats at St. Peter's, walking meditation is included in the day. It is a wonderful practice, and you would be amazed at what can be seen as you walk very slowly through the cemetery at the church.

But my chief practice of Simply Being is the discipline of Centering Prayer. Centering Prayer is simply the intention to consent to the presence and action of God within. It is the practice of letting go, self-emptying, and it is not easy. But it is said by some to be Jesus' core practice. It is embedded in the Philippians text read on Palm Sunday—"...who did not count equality with God a thing to be grasped but emptied himself taking on the form of a servant..." (Philippians 2:3-8). It is not an easy practice because each of us is so steeped in our culture's demand that we take, hold on, hoard. We don't let go, become empty. Cynthia Bourgeault, who has written extensively about Centering Prayer, calls it contemplation, not meditation, because, she says, contemplative prayer means that one is caught, held from the other side, like dancing with a partner. Contemplation, she says, is a deeply relational practice.

Richard Rohr in his book, *The Universal Christ*, offers a number of Simply Being practices. One is called "Simply That You Are." It entails focusing not on your differences from God, but that you are joined to God through grace. It encourages you to see that what matters isn't *what* you are, but *that* you are, and that this is enough.

Simply that you are! Your own body, in its naked being with no "doing" involved, becomes the place of revelation and inner rest. Christ becomes despiritualized.

We Are in Desperate Need

*In those days, John the Baptist
appeared in the wilderness of Judea,
proclaiming, "Repent, for the
kingdom of heaven has come near."*
Matthew 3:1-2

THE ADMONITION, "CARLYLE, BE A LADY," WAS MY MOTHER'S mantra. She said it on almost any occasion. I'm sure she believed that if she said it often enough, I would, in fact, become a lady. A lady had good table manners. She wrote short, prompt thank-you notes. She never said what she thought—even if she knew. And God forbid she should say what she felt—even if she knew. A lady was placid, quiet, helpful, and proper. Never assertive or aggressive. Never passionate or on fire about anything.

John the Baptist, the central character in the gospel this morn-ing on the second Sunday in the season of Advent, was not a lady. Or a gentleman. John the Baptist was on fire. He was passionate about the presence and reality of God. He gave up good food, nice clothes, comfortable living quarters—everything—to be the voice of fire and passion for the presence and action of God in the world. He was especially intent on putting a fire under the religious people of the day, those who practiced the right rituals but had no passion for the presence and action of God in the world. Those who, in the words of the prophet Amos, would sell the needy for a pair of sandals.

Because John had given up so much of his world and his religion's trappings, he was no longer anesthetized, no longer asleep, no longer inured to the world's sufferings, to what had happened to God's good creation. And he wasn't afraid to say so in the starkest of terms. He called the religious people who gathered at his river pulpit "a brood of vipers." Calling one's congregation a snake pit wouldn't endear a preacher then or now. He told them that God had no use for their traditions, that God could raise up from these stones children of Abraham! He told them that they too had to let it all go and start anew, not just say they were sorry and tweak a few behaviors here and there. But repent. Turn around. Radically change. See what was going on around them, in their midst, where they were, in fact, complicit. He expected that the messiah for whom they all longed would come with fire and judgment.

"I baptize you with water," he said, "but the one who comes will baptize you with the holy spirit and with fire" (Matthew 3: 11-13).

Many of us would like to skip over John the Baptist and this second Sunday in the season of Advent. Let's get back to the beautiful candles, to the quiet (ladylike) preparation for

Jesus' birth. We are uncomfortable around this eccentric, loud, passionate, fiery prophet.

Years ago, when I was at St. Alban's parish in Washington, D.C., I dressed up like John the Baptist on this Sunday. I found an old raggedy black wig with gnarled curls that hung down to my shoulders. I couldn't find sackcloth and ashes, but I found an equally tattered and unattractive outfit. I looked bad, really bad. I stood in the narthex before the service preparing to sing the *Godspell* tune, "Prepare Ye the Way of the Lord." No one, not one person, spoke to me. Not one of the hundreds of people who passed by me recognized me. I imagine people thought I was one of the regular homeless people who showed up on Sunday morning to get a handout. Until I began walking down the center aisle, singing, no one knew me or cared to know me.

This week I came upon a conversation going on in the Episcopal Café, the on-line Episcopal church blog. It is about whether Advent is a time of repentance or not. A well-known theologian says Advent is not such a time, that the church needs to get away from judgment and penitence. It drives people away. The responding bloggers have taken issue and say that this is indeed a time of judgment and penitence.

Actually, I don't need a blog to agree with the repentance bloggers. All I need to do is go to the movies at Midway. That will do it. Have you seen "Twelve Years a Slave"? Talk about the need for repentance. Or "The Dallas Buyers' Club"? After seeing these two movies, I felt like I had been to the river listening to

John the Baptist. We are, each of us, in desperate need of repentance, turning around, seeing, changing how we treat each other, ourselves, and all of God's good creation. We are in desperate need of becoming passionate and fiery about what we see.

On my car there is a magnet that reads, "LOVE GOD, LOVE YOUR NEIGHBOR. CHANGE THE WORLD." A friend recently saw this and said, "Carlyle, don't you think that's a little too evangelical?" Read "unladylike." "No," I wanted to scream. "That's exactly what the world needs now."

John, passionate, fiery John, prepared the way. The One who came, baptized with the Holy Spirit and with fire but with a different fire—the fire of love. The kind of love that welcomes anyone from a profligate son to a despised tax collector, to a woman of the city (definitely not a lady), to a self-righteous Pharisee, to you, and to me. That kind of love can take our breath away, if not our complacent blindness. That kind of love can turn us around, save our souls, our very lives.

Learn to See, To Really See

*There was a rich man who was
dressed in purple and fine linen
and who feasted sumptuously every
day.*
Luke 16:19

SOME OF US, WHEN ASKED, MIGHT SAY WE COME TO CHURCH FOR comfort—some kind of consoling word in our lives of distress and difficulty of one kind or another. But if we came today looking for comfort, we picked the wrong Sunday! Today's gospel is loaded with judgment. No gentle Jesus meek and mild here! Actually, I don't know where that picture of Jesus came from—clearly not from the gospel stories. Perhaps this picture is our way to try to tame Jesus, for there is judgment lurking in almost all of Jesus' parables.

Think of the judgment leveled at the clergy who crossed to the other side of the road in the parable of the good Samaritan. Or the judgment leveled at the older son who was too absorbed in his own self-righteousness to have compassion for his younger brother in the parable of the prodigal son. Or the judgment leveled at Simon the Pharisee who cannot see the woman of the city who crashed his dinner party. There is judgment lurking in all of Jesus' parables.

But today it doesn't just lurk. Judgment is front and center—clear and unmistakable and not to be missed. This judgment is about wealth and the disparities wealth can create. Issues around wealth hit close to home for us because this is where many of us actually live and move and have our being. Wealth is something many of us value highly, and it separates us from those who have less.

This parable about the disparities and separations caused by wealth plays out in the halls of Congress as we speak. We don't want to provide food stamps for "a-bods," right? That would be able-bodied people even though they may, through no fault of their own, be under-employed or still suffering from the economic collapse. A collapse, by the way, not caused by them but by wealthy Wall Street traders who wanted to amass more wealth at any cost.

Jesus, in this morning's parable, paints in graphic terms the disparities between the rich man and Lazarus. The rich man is clothed in purple, the color of wealth. Lazarus is clothed in sores that the dogs lick. The rich man is well-fed, fat and happy. Lazarus only yearns for crumbs, the trash that might fall from the rich man's table. The rich man never actually sees Lazarus, even though he must step over him to leave his gated community.

They each die in true parabolic fashion—in a great reversal

of fortune. The rich man goes to Hades, and Lazarus goes to the arms of Abraham where he is finally well cared for. The rich man learns what most of us fear somewhere deep in our psyches—there are consequences, but we learn them after it's too late to do anything about them. At least, the rich man says, warn my brothers and even, in his absolute blindness, urges Lazarus to do his bidding. Still ordering people around, even from Hades.

The parable shows us the great chasm between the two men. The truth, however, is that the chasm existed long, long before they died. The chasm was there in their day-to-day lives. The rich man could not, would not, did not see Lazarus, and that is the real issue.

Chasm is another word for separation, and separation is actually the root of the word sin. This story is about the sin that keeps us from *seeing* each other, seeing which might actually prevent us from stepping over each other. This theme is at the heart of most of Jesus' parables. The clergy cannot and will not see the man in the ditch. The older son cannot and will not see his younger brother. Simon cannot and will not see the woman at his dinner party. Jesus even asks Simon pointedly, "Do you see this woman?" (Luke 7:44).

Many members of Congress cannot and will not see the millions of Americans who cannot afford the high cost of food for their families. But they have no trouble seeing and complaining about the impact of no health care subsidies on their own health insurance policies.

But so that this sermon is not a rant about Congress, let me tell you a brief personal story. A friend and I went out for dinner in Silver Spring. Silver Spring, like much of the Washington area, is gentrifying. The place we went for dinner was not as gentrified as most. On our way to the restaurant, a woman approached us, calling out to us. When we turned around, we saw a woman obviously very poor, probably living on the streets, looking way older than her years, with two shopping bags full of her possessions. I stopped, fumbling in my purse for money to give her. My friend walked on. Then I walked on too. I'm not sure what the right thing was to do in that situation. But at the very least, we should have engaged her, acknowledged her presence.

It reminds me of a story that C.S. Lewis tells of being stopped by a beggar who asked for money. Lewis' friend said, "Don't give that guy money. He'll only go to a bar and have a drink." Lewis responded, "That, sir, is just what I was going to do." I have not forgotten that woman on the street in Silver Spring, and I regret that I did nothing. There was a chasm between us. I feel Jesus' judgment.

Jesus' judgment comes from a profound awareness that we are one in God—all of us. Rich and poor, old and young, white/brown/black, male and female, gay and straight. Jesus' judgment comes from a profound awareness that God's yearning in creation, God's intention, is that we know and experience our oneness with God and all of creation. That is why when asked for the bottom line, Jesus says, "Love the Lord your God with all your heart and love your neighbor as yourself" (Matthew 22:37-39). In other words, we are one.

But how will we ever know and experience this oneness? How will we ever learn to be, to act from it? How will the chasms of all of our lives really be healed? How will we ever learn to really see? These are the core questions.

Gordon Cosby, founder of the Church of the Savior in Washington, D.C., whose ministry is largely to the Lazaruses of the world, said this: "Who am I? Beneath all other answers, I am in Christ. I am immersed in God's nature. Christ's nature has permeated and inserted itself into my deepest being. That is my core identity." That comment reminded me of communion, communion here at St. Peter's. It is almost as though we say at the altar rail, "The body of Christ for the Body of Christ." It is here at this altar rail that we are reminded of our core identity. We, you and I, *are* the Body of Christ. We, you and I, are immersed in the oneness of God, in God's being.

The 15th century author of *The Cloud of Unknowing*, a spiritual classic, says this: "God is your being, and what you are, you are in God." So, if we came to St. Peter's this morning for communion, we are in the right place. God, in Christ, steps over all chasms to be with us, in us. May we, then, each of us, learn to live from that place of communion.

False Piety

*Remember that you are dust, and
to dust you shall return.*
Genesis 3:19

THESE ARE THE STARK WORDS THAT ARE SAID TO EACH OF US as the ashen cross is marked on our foreheads. Who wants to remember that? Isn't our life's project forgetting that?

These words remind us that we are limited, that our lives will end, that all we have worked so hard to accomplish in ourselves, our families, our jobs, will come to a close. These words from the Ash Wednesday service remind us of the fact that we are human, humus, made of the earth, and to the earth we shall return. These Ash Wednesday words remind us that we are not in control. We did not bring ourselves into being, and we do not know when we will die.

For most of us, this is not good news. We want to act as if or at least believe that this reality is not true of us. We are special. We are moving toward greater perfection. Or, if not that, we can at least fool the people around us into believing it's so.

There are many ways we struggle with our humanness, our essential weakness, imperfection, and mortality. One might say that addiction in whatever form it takes is an attempt to fill, cover over, help us forget who we really are. Barbara Brown Taylor says that 99% of us are addicted to something, whether it's eating, shopping, blaming, or taking care of other people. Not to mention the other addictions—to alcohol, drugs, and work.

Ash Wednesday, the beginning of Lent, reminds us of another, very insidious way of dealing with our humanity and mortality—piety. False piety is the discipline of specialness. Look at me! Look at what I do! Look at my special relationship with God! All of which implies that I am better than you are. I am spiritual. God even likes me more than you! Think about the Pharisee who says, "Thank God I am not like that tax collector!" False piety is a well-trod path of trying to forget that we are dust and to dust we shall return.

But it doesn't work. It isn't a real relationship with God because we are not real.

We are invited, however, to a holy Lent, not to a pious Lent, with this very recognition—that we are dust and to dust we shall return. That we are limited, frail, vulnerable, human.

And, this knowledge has its graces. First of all, it is the truth, in the starkest of terms. Nothing—not money, power, prestige, or piety—can take this reality away. Nothing can erase the fact of our mortality. No amount of mind-numbing addictions can remove our dusty natures. But this knowledge is more than truth.

Our very humanity, our frailty, is the very opening for God's real presence in our lives.

Franciscan Richard Rohr says it best when he describes that refusing to acknowledge our vulnerability is like trying to attach two inflated balloons to each other. They simply will not stick together. But when the risen Christ reveals his human wounds, he links himself to our experiences and allows us to own our suffering as well.

You and I can leave St. Peter's today practicing our false piety before others by allowing the ashes on our foreheads to show others that we have done our duty and have been to an Ash Wednesday service. Or we can leave here today knowing the truth about ourselves and allowing that truth to open us to the living presence of God in our lives.

Remember that you are dust, and to dust you shall return. And remember that God meets you there. Just there.

Blindness to Wrongs

*Some people brought a blind man to him
and begged him to touch him. He took the
blind man by the hand and led him out
of the village; and when he had put saliva
on his eyes and laid his hands on him, he
asked him, "Can you see anything?"*
Mark 8:22-23

For Lutherans, today is Reformation Sunday, always the
last Sunday in October, as I am told by my Lutheran colleagues.
However, for me, it is Transformation Sunday. Luther's way of
getting to reformation was by grace alone, and it is mine also.
But my way may have a bit of a theological kitchen sink quality
because I want to talk about suffering, healing, compassion, transformation, and following—otherwise known as mission. That's a
theological kitchen sink mouthful!

Here goes. The first thing to know about the gospel text
this morning is that Mark has a very clever and sometimes
obscure way of making a point. The academic exegetes call his
technique a "Markan Sandwich." Think of a sandwich shop like

Subway or Arena's. When Mark wants to make an important point, he frames the point with stories about blindness, each story one slice of bread. So, there's the first piece of bread that is the story of the blind man at Bethsaida that we heard in September, and the second slice of bread is today's story about the blind beggar, Bartimaeus. The meat in the middle? These are the stories we've been hearing lately about the disciples—Peter, James, and John.

Peter does not want to hear anything about Jesus' suffering and death. James and John want to know who will be the greatest and, barring that, who will sit at the right and the left. The meat of this story, then, is about the disciples, those closest to Jesus, who do not want to talk about suffering and death. Glory to them is greatness. Glory to Jesus is self-emptying, letting go, and the acknowledgment and acceptance of suffering and death. Mark's question is, then, who is really blind?

I get it. Many of us have been raised to be just like Peter, James, and John. We don't want to talk about suffering. Some of us can't even acknowledge it. Someone asks, "How are you?" And we answer, "I'm fine," even if we are totally miserable. That's very understandable. Most of us were raised in homes where difficult things could not be talked about, much less felt.

But suffering is a real and very important part of the human condition. It's just true. We suffer because we are limited, frail human beings. We cannot control the world, most especially our own worlds and those of the ones we love.

The next portion of this homily was to be an example from my own life, how personal suffering has often been an unexpected, grace-filled gift. But yesterday's events and those of this past week have superseded my life.

Our country is suffering. The hatred that drove someone to send bombs all over our country to individuals he disagreed with and despised. The hatred that drove someone to kill eleven people at worship in the Tree of Life Synagogue in Pittsburgh. This is suffering. Great suffering. For those threatened. For those wounded and killed and their families. For the law enforcement people who responded to the events. For the perpetrators. And for ourselves as we try to understand how this could happen here.

I do not know what the grace will be, what the grace can be, but I do know that we ignore our country's suffering and the hatred that is propelling it, and we ignore it to our peril.

Mark's gospel is apt for this Sunday. Perhaps the real grace in our situation is the recognition that we cannot remain blind to our country's suffering. For Mark, the one who truly sees is Bartimaeus. As a blind beggar left by the side of the road, he has suffered. He is open and ready for Jesus. "What do you want?" Jesus asks. "Let me see again," Bartimaeus immediately responds (Mark 10:51). He is willing, willing to see and therefore willing to follow.

Seeing is not always easy, but blindness can be catastrophic. We have seen what blindness can do in our world.

I would like to end this sermon with some silence, a time to hold our suffering, our country's suffering. A time to pray for healing.

Yes, It's a Journey

When they heard the king, they set out;
and there, ahead of them went the star that
they had seen at its rising until it stopped
over the place where the child was.
Matthew 2:9

ACTUALLY, IT'S ABOUT THE SPIRITUAL JOURNEY, THIS GOSPEL WE hear this morning. It's important to look closely at it, to rescue it from its comfortable, sentimental, overdone, and over-known aspects because it's a great story about the spiritual journey, a journey every one of us is on.

So, yes, it's a journey. Sometimes it takes a long time. Sometimes we have to come from very far away like the wise men in this morning's gospel. The terrain can be difficult, and there are detours, unexpected adventures, sore feet, sore souls, sadness, pain, disappointment, and loss. Sometimes we are tempted to give up and go back to where we thought we were comfortable, but we drag on because, well, because something is drawing us onward. Probably the wise men in today's story were from somewhere in or near Iraq. They walked, say, from Baghdad to Jerusalem and on to Bethlehem. If you've ever been in that part of the world, you know just how difficult that journey was. No Southwest Air, no Airtrans, no Greyhound buses. Only feet. Only slow movement. Spiritual writers across the centuries have described this journey. St. Augustine of Hippo put it this way over 1,600 years ago—"Our hearts are restless until they find rest in Thee." A contemporary writer says, "The foundational assumption is that union with God is not something we are trying to acquire; God is already the ground of our being. It is a question of realizing this in our lives…. God is our homeland." Yet, it can take a long time, a long journey to come home.

One of the very great aspects to this morning's gospel is the announcement, the wonderful announcement implicit in it, that everyone, EVERYONE, is invited on this journey! These wise men were not Jews. They were Persians, probably practitioners of Zoroastrianism. They were astrologers, the scientists of their day. They were not orthodox religious people. They were seekers. They paid attention to the signs, to their dreams, to their innards. This is fabulous news for all of us. We do not need to have the right religion, the right set of beliefs, or belong to the right denomination to be on this most important journey. All we have to do is to be willing to say "Yes" at some level to the summons home. As Dag Hammarskjöld once said, "I don't know who put the question or when, but I know at some point I said 'Yes'." Much of this world's strife would be over if we could just accept that, in the end, we are all on the same journey home.

Yet this spiritual journey is not without its danger. Matthew clearly includes the dark and foreboding danger lurking in this story. Herod will stop at nothing to preserve his power. He even murdered two of his own sons so that he could stay in power! He ordered the murder of infants under the age of two just to get rid of the supposed threat of a little baby in a small out-of-the-way country town called Bethlehem.

There is danger here. No, we don't have a Herod looking over our shoulders, but we do live in a culture, we swim in a worldview, that does not want us to see or partake in the transforming power of the spiritual life. We live in a culture that denies this reality as fantasy at best. Our culture bids us do homage to the economy. The true god is money, stuff, possessions, and power. The discovery of our real homeland, the God of our being, the God of love, is a true threat to the false gods embedded in our culture.

This journey is dangerous because this spiritual journey is transforming. It upends our worldview, our values, our behaviors. There is a great book by the neurosurgeon Eben Alexander called *Proof of Heaven*. Alexander had a near-death experience from bacterial meningitis, something most people do not survive. He was a confirmed skeptic, a scientist who didn't believe in other realities, but he countenanced them when his patients described them. He thought he had answers for everything until he almost died. In the course of that experience, he reports hearing the voice of God who said to him, "You are loved and cherished. You have nothing to fear. There is nothing you can do wrong." When writing about this experience, Alexander says, "If I had to boil this entire message down to one sentence it would run this way: You are loved. And if I had to boil it down further to just one word, it would (of course) be simply, Love."

Dr. Eben Alexander was transformed. He knew it would be difficult to tell his colleagues about this experience. He knew that there would be many who would try to invalidate it. But he knows now that it is his duty to talk about it, to write about it. He says, "Not only was my journey about love, but it was also about who we are and how connected we are all are—the very meaning of all existence."

This journey, this spiritual journey, is not only transforming, it is literally **en**-lightening. There is a good reason that there is so much emphasis on light during this season called Epiphany. The wise men followed light because it was there, this light, embedded in all things and in each of us. Have you ever noticed how in some paintings and icons the light is not from the outside but from the inside? This is the unbearable lightness of being, the Godly ground of our being, in all things and in all persons. The bible calls this light glory, or *kabod* in Hebrew. Its meaning is in the sanctus we say every Sunday—Holy, Holy, Holy. Having had tastes of these experiences myself, I can say AMEN, which in Hebrew literally means YES.

Finally, it is important to say that the spiritual journey, the journey to our homeland in God, is here and now, not then and there. The biblical story is important. It provides clues, metaphors, and openings. But the journey is not then and there. It is here and now, for each of us.

Conspirators All

When he had said this, he breathed on them
and said to them, "Receive the Holy Spirit."
John 20:22

MY SERMON BEGINS WITH A LITTLE HOMILETICAL PROLEGOMENA. This is Pentecost Sunday, when we celebrate the gift of the spirit and the formation of the church. The schema we follow comes from what is called Luke-Acts. The liturgical year, using Luke-Acts, celebrates Easter, and then, fifty days later, Pentecost. The gospel of John, however, sees it differently and locates Easter and Pentecost in the same moments, not separated by fifty days. My homily follows John's schema because it makes more sense to me. As you will soon hear, I love John's story of the risen Jesus' appearance to the sacred disciples locked away in the upper room. There is something powerfully intimate about Jesus breathing on those sacred, huddled people. This little prolegomena is simply meant to locate us in John's narrative about Pentecost and not Luke's.

Long ago, someone at St. Alban's said to me, "Carlyle, I think

God is wonderful. I think the Holy Spirit is lovely. But Jesus— Jesus—I have trouble with Jesus!"

I offered a pastoral response, something like "Hmm…" or "Uh-huh." But the author of John's gospel—let's just call him John—has a much more effective response.

John would have said, and in fact says, "Oh no. No. There is no dividing up the presence of God. This whole energetic from-beginning-to-end is about oneness. One. And there is no way you can have a preference for a part of something that is not divisible."

That would have been a pastoral, theological, prophetic, and very truthful response. Far more helpful than my "Hmm…" or "Uh-huh."

Well, of course. John's understanding, John's theology, which is brilliant, poetic, and, well, fabulous, is about oneness from beginning to end. Creation, Incarnation, Crucifixion, Resurrection, and Holy Spirit are—or, shall I say is—a seamless flow. It is no accident that John's gospel begins with Genesis, "In the beginning." The author of all creation, John tells us, became flesh—a person, incarnate, like you and me. "In the beginning was the Word and the Word was made flesh and dwelt among us full of grace and truth" (John 1:1). And after breaking the bonds of death, he walked through the upper room door to greet those cowering disciples with "peace be with you." And then he *breathed* on them and said, "Receive the holy spirit" (John 20:22).

Jesus breathed on them. Breath. In Hebrew it is *ruach* for wind or *nephesh* for life. In Greek it is *pneuma*. It is God's *ruach* that hovers over the chaos. Creation, Incarnation, Resurrection, gift of the Spirit. One seamless flow. To us.

Breath. We are all breathing as I speak. I am breathing as I speak. There are no words without breath. They are formed from breath. Breath is so intimate. We only hear each other breathe when we are close enough to detect such a faint sound. Without breath, we die.

Jesus breathed on them and said, "Receive the Holy Spirit." Just did it. Passed on the breath of creation, incarnation, and resurrection, infusing them with life, new life. Breath. In one breath, they received it all.

This is what we remember today. Not just remember as if we are looking at the upper room scrap book, but remember as in *re*-member. As in know that we—you and I—are breathed upon, put back together, given new life. *RE*-membered.

You see, the church, born at Pentecost with what John says is Jesus' very breath, is essentially a conspiracy. To conspire literally means to breathe together. We are not building, a denomination or a creed. We are a conspiracy.

The earliest friends of Jesus became conspirators of forgiveness. What a radical act! A gift of new life, new breath. Jesus said, "Receive the Holy Spirit. If you forgive the sins of any, they are forgiven them. If you retain the sins of any, they are retained." Think about this in your life. Think about the impact forgiveness can have. What happens when we hold on to stuff? What happens when we let go? This is the first conspiracy of what we call church.

Forgiveness. And we—all of us, not just clergy—have been given the power to forgive, to let go, to restore to life, to wholeness, to well-being.

A Stephen Minister who listens, simply listens, conspires. Listening, really listening, is a lost art in our culture. We live in a culture of noise and babble, a culture that values who can shout the loudest. A Stephen minister participates in the breath of God simply by listening deeply. Ditto for the youth group minister or Godly Play teacher. Conspirators. Really being with children, no matter what. In January, after the tragic death of Mende George, Jeffrey and Mark went to be with the children to talk about death and grief. Conspiring. Participating in the breath of God.

Conspirators. Those who hunger and thirst for righteousness' sake, whether at the community resource center or caring for those trapped in poverty. Those who are working to expose and undermine systemic racism in our community. Those who feed the hungry or sit with the dying or listen to the suffering. Conspirators, all.

But like breathing, we are hardly aware of our conspiracies. And that's just as well, because otherwise our conspiracies become acts of hubris.

So, every once in a while take a deep breath and hear Jesus' words. "Receive the holy spirit."

Then, conspire.

Peculiar Treasures

*He is able to deal gently with the
ignorant and wayward, since he
himself is subject to weakness.*
Hebrews 5:2

EMBEDDED IN THE GOSPEL OF JOHN'S STORY ABOUT NICODEMUS
is this: "The spirit blows where it will. We hear the sound of it
but we do not know where it comes from or where it is going."
We often don't even know it's blowing except in that great opti-
cal opportunity called twenty-twenty hindsight. But today, this
Sunday, at this very moment, we can at least catch a glimpse of it
in our midst. There is too much coincidence today to be merely
coincidence. The spirit is blowing—right here, this day—at St.
Peter's By-the-Sea in Lewes, Delaware.

How do we know? It's in the epistle for today from Hebrews.
Now I know we don't often focus on the epistle, but today the spirit has sneaked into it for us. I don't think I've ever used this epistle
as a preaching text. The epistle to the Hebrews, usually attributed
to St. Paul, is basically a sermon to a struggling congregation.

This early church is in trouble. Attendance is declining. There is theological confusion. "Just who is this Jesus anyway? What did he do for us? Can you tell us again? And, please, what is this perfect offering, sacrifice-for-sin stuff all about? We aren't blind! Sin is still alive and well."

Let's assume now that St. Paul did write this epistle. He had *lots* of experience with struggling congregations. Today he might be among the most sought-after church consultants! His letters—most of the epistles in the New Testament—are written to congregations he founded. No sooner did he walk out the door after getting them organized than they fell into trouble—arguing with one another, forming cliques, engaging in theological squabbles of all sorts. Just read his letters to the church at Corinth. What a mess! If we think the Anglican Communion of today is in trouble, we have only to read this series of letters to Corinth. Paul finally had enough when the Corinthians started competing with one another over who was the most spiritually gifted and which of these gifts was best. The text read at weddings—often without knowing its context—sets the record straight on this issue. Love is the greatest spiritual gift beside which all others pale.

All of this makes great sense to me. One of the things I love most about scripture is its incarnate, gritty, very human, and very messy quality. How we even got to this stained-glass view of holy scripture I'll never understand because the Bible is full of people who make mistakes, sometimes big ones. People who commit adultery, who lie, who cheat and steal, who are constantly competing with one another over who is the greatest among them. People who are generally rather limited, often broken people, who are the very people God loves, whom God yearns to be in relationship with, whom God calls, and calls beloved. At one point in scripture God calls us "peculiar treasures."

And the church itself—a gathering of these same peculiar treasures—is just as incarnational, gritty, human, and messy. And that, my beloved friends, is why we are here at St. Peter's By-the-Sea in Lewes, Delaware. We are not that much different from that early church community who were the original recipients of today's epistle. We too struggle with theological questions. What is it that Jesus did for us, please? We struggle with community concerns.

The reason the spirit is so evidently at work today is that we are experiencing a match between the "then" story contained in today's epistle to the Hebrews and our "now" story here at St. Peter's. It is annual meeting Sunday when we focus on our life in community. What does the author of the epistle to the Hebrews say to that congregation and thus to us through the wind, the mediation of the spirit?

The core theology in this epistle is this: God incarnate came into the gritty messiness of life in the person of Jesus of Nazareth, into our midst, to help us see in the flesh that God's ultimate yearning is to be in a loving relationship with us no matter who we are, no matter how we are, willing to suffer from who and how we are. God-in-the-flesh joined us not to fix our lives, not to take away our pain and suffering, but to enter deeply and completely into them, to take them on, to be Emmanuel, God with us. Embedded in this epistle is a most radical understanding of Jesus—that the person of Jesus is God incarnate precisely because Jesus embraced the essential weakness and vulnerability of what it means to be human. This is the love of God, the essential work of God, to come this close to us, to be with us where it matters most. To be with us in weakness, in vulnerability, in suffering, and in death. In other words, where the rubber meets the proverbial road.

In another epistle, Paul says that the work of the community called church is to grow into the full stature of Christ. If that is so, then our work is to embrace our humanity—our essential vulnerability, brokenness, and weakness—knowing that precisely there God is with us. Emmanuel.

I have often thought that the community called church really should be renamed "a school for lovers," because that is what we are learning here—how to love ourselves and each other within the loving embrace of a God who meets us where we are. The very curriculum for this "school for lovers," includes our difficulties, challenges, and suffering. We can do that here because the one who gathers us knows this syllabus inside and out.

As we deal with our own challenges here at St. Peter's—our own suffering, vulnerability, questions, concerns, and difficulties—it is important to remember that no one ever said it was easy or should be so. It is part of the suchness (as the Buddhists would say) of community. What is most important is to remember that we are not in it alone. And that learning to live in community, in the wide embrace of a God who is with us, is all part of our individual and corporate growing up into the full stature of Christ. There are no finished products among us, not one. We are all a people on the way and of the way.

Nothing But the Love in Our Hearts

*After this, the Lord appointed
seventy others and sent them on
ahead of him in pairs to every
town and place where he himself
intended to go.*
Luke 10:1

HAVE YOU EVER WONDERED ABOUT THE DIALOGUE THAT IS
not included in the gospel stories? Like the gospel story this
morning? Don't you imagine some of those seventy people had a
thing or two to say to Jesus? "What? No purse? No sandals? No
bag? Are you kidding? I never go anywhere without my purse!"
Or something like, "So, no purse, no bag, no sandals, and you're
sending me out like a lamb in the midst of wolves? I don't think
so." "Sending me out empty-handed? No training? Not even a
weekend retreat?"

I don't know if there was any of that dialogue, but I can't
imagine not asking a few of those questions. Yet it does appear
that Jesus was sending out those seventy empty-handed. If we
published sermon titles on the sign at the corner of Market and

Second, this one might be called "Empty-handed Ministry," since it looks like that's just what Jesus meant.

One of my "unfounded in actual fact" theories about the origin of ordination is that empty-handed ministry is just too anxiety provoking for most. We need training. We need skills. We need certification. We can't just go out there with nothing, no purse, no bag, no sandals. Besides, we don't just need sandals, we need a shirt and collar, right?

Similarly, baptism is not just an invitation to empty-handed ministry but a kind of spiritual insurance policy that promises us that we will be on the fast track to heaven should anything untoward happen to us and our children. Baptism and ordination cloak us in safety. They are not sacraments that initiate us into risk, into empty-handed ministry.

But you ask any ordained person or any baptized person who is willing to be honest and they will tell you that no amount of information, training, degree, collar or shirt, sandals, purse, or bag actually contributes to empty-handed ministry, to proclaiming that the kingdom is near. Because proclaiming that the kingdom is near actually means *being* the kingdom, walking the walk.

I had my first taste of empty-handed ministry before I went to seminary. It should have been a big eye-opener to this ministry thing. I was twenty-five and in a chaplaincy training program at Mass General Hospital in Boston. I was told to visit a woman who was dying and who desperately wanted answers to her questions. "Why is this happening to me?" she demanded to know. I didn't have a clue, but I thought I *should* know so I said something like, "Well, God loves you anyway." I'm surprised she didn't leap out of bed and throw me across the room. Today I would tell her that I don't have an answer to that question as well as a host of other questions. But I would be happy to sit with her—empty-handed.

Many years later I was the rector of an Episcopal church in Washington, D.C., squarely in the middle of one of the city's largest crack cocaine drug markets. St. Stephen's was a perfect place to sell drugs because it occupied a large part of a city block and was empty and dark every night. After a man was shot and killed on our front steps—a drug deal gone bad—the parish administrator told me she was going to sit outside on the steps with the drug dealers. What??? I told her in no uncertain terms that she wasn't. She was the mother of two small children and expecting her third. She said, "No, I am going to sit outside with the drug dealers." "Okay," I said, "I'm sitting with you." The two of us put up metal folding chairs and sat outside with the dealers. You can imagine how unhappy this made them. A pregnant woman and a cleric on metal folding chairs. Gradually more and more parishioners joined us. The choir even began to rehearse on the steps. Neighbors started to join us. Children— many children—came out to play at night while we sat there. We got to know some of the drug dealers and their families. That portion of Newton St. in northwest Washington gradually changed. We had nothing but folding chairs and a little courage.

No, it didn't end drug dealing in that part of the city, but some glimmer of the kingdom was seen.

About a month ago I gathered with five other people around a dying woman. In fact, she gathered us. It was an incredible occasion. Everyone present was empty-handed. I actually have never felt so empty-handed. There was nothing we could do to prevent her death. No one could fix it. No one had any answer for it, and no one tried. No one turned away from the reality of this woman's suffering and dying. We were with her—empty-handed. The love in the living room the afternoon we celebrated the Eucharist together was powerful enough to blow the walls out in every direction. I imagine it felt the same way in that upper room at the last supper.

So, it's true. You and I are called to get out there with nothing—no purse, no bag, no sandals—nothing but the love in our hearts. We are called to be there, to be Jesus' people, to be present, to demonstrate that the kingdom is near. All we need is the grace to be empty-handed.

Intimacy and Doubt

*So the other disciples told him, "We
have seen the Lord." But he said to
them, "Unless I see the mark of the
nails in his hands, and put my finger
in the mark of the nails and my hand
in his side, I will not believe."*
John 20:25

THIS SUNDAY IS TYPICALLY CALLED "DOUBTING THOMAS
Sunday." I don't think doubt is the issue, though. I think it's
fear of intimacy. Many of us don't want to be close to Jesus. I
often think of a person I knew at St. Alban's in D.C. who said,
"I have no problem with God. I think the Holy Spirit is lovely.
But Jesus, Jesus. I have trouble with Jesus."

I think the real issue with Jesus, the most difficult issue, is not
the resurrection but the wide-open invitation to intimacy that this
man kept and keeps offering. It's hard for us to bear. We tend to
keep to ourselves, keep our troubles to ourselves. We are trained
not to let anyone see our wounds, not to mention inviting anyone
into them. And therefore, we cannot see the wounds of others.

I have been looking at the 17th century painter Caravaggio's rendition of this text. It is an extraordinary work of art. Jesus bends toward Thomas, and Jesus takes Thomas' hand and guides it into his side, into his open wound. The brightest light in the painting is on Jesus' breast as he opens his clothes, revealing the wound in his side. It's an amazing sight, so tender, so intimate.

This painting depicts an incredible invitation to intimacy. Actually, the earliest name for this Sunday was not "Doubting Thomas Sunday" but "Incredulous Thomas Sunday." Who wouldn't be incredulous that someone brutally killed and alive again would guide your hand into his wound? Yes, Thomas asks to see, but Jesus goes way beyond sight. He takes Thomas' hand and gently guides it into his open side. It's no wonder many of us have trouble with Jesus. We may not want to get that close, to feel his wounds.

But the author of this gospel warned us in chapter one that this was the word made flesh. And flesh we got. This is a fleshy, intimacy-inviting Jesus. We should all be squirming by now.

I think doubt actually protects us from this Jesus. We want to push away that inviting hand and not get too close. Because if we let that hand guide us to that wound, what will happen to us? What then? Or, put another way, if someone loves us that much to say, "Touch me, hold me," what will we do?

There is nothing wrong with doubting, and there is much to question in our time. Jesus himself asked more questions than he answered and harshly critiqued his own faith tradition. But there may be times when doubting is a way of protecting ourselves from the intimate Jesus, protecting us from love.

If we say "Yes" to the hand that stretches out to us, what will that mean? What will that ask of us? If we allow Jesus' hand to guide our own hands to the wounds of the world, what difference might that make?

I believe Caravaggio's painting may be perfect for our time. We live in a very wounded time. It is perhaps no more so than other times, but this is our time. There are wounds abounding.

Each one of us lives with wounds, from childhood, from loss, from dreams deferred, from the inevitable decline and death. For many of us, these wounds are hard to face, hard to touch. Our society lives with incredible wounds, the wounds of poverty and prejudice.

I have been thinking a lot about Dr. Martin Luther King, Jr., as I imagine you have also. He was killed fifty years and four days ago. He was killed because he dared to name the wounds, see the wounds, and feel the wounds that racism, poverty, and war have inflicted on all of us. He saw and named the hatred that inflicted these wounds, and he would not stop talking and preaching about it. And like the hand of Jesus in Caravaggio's painting, he lovingly led our hands into these wounds. He was killed because he was unafraid to name and feel the wounds of racism, poverty, and injustice.

I believe Dr. King's faith gave him the courage to name and touch these wounds. The biblical stories of exodus from bondage and victory over death gave him hope—the kind of hope that propelled him to act, to care, to love.

John Paul Sartre defined courage as "living to the point of tears." I believe this is Jesus' invitation to us this Easter. To allow his hand to guide our hands to his side, to his wounds, to feel and know the wounds of the world and to act with the same love that comes to us from that gentle, guiding hand.

The Inescapable God

Where can I go from your spirit? Or
where can I flee from your presence?
Psalm 139:7

THE HEBREW SCRIPTURE AND GOSPEL TEXTS TODAY ARE ABOUT call. So perhaps we might say that the season of Epiphany is something like a "let's get on with it" time. Yahweh is ready to roll. Jesus is ready to roll. He's calling companions, asking them to follow.

Call stories abound in the biblical story. The boy Samuel is called by God, not by Eli, and he eventually answers, "Here I am, for you called me" (1 Samuel 3:4). The hymn verse, "Here I am Lord, I have heard you calling in the night," is sung heartily in seminary communities and churches.

But Samuel's call is just the beginning of a very difficult story. He is called to give bad news to the old man Eli and his debauched sons. He is called to anoint the first king over Israel, Saul, and kings don't work out so well in the end. And Samuel's own family has its problems. His sons turn out no better than Eli's.

In the gospel call story, Nathaniel asks, "Can anything good come out of Israel?" (John 1:46). Was it sarcasm or a genuine question? For the author of the gospel, the question continues to make the point that "the word was made flesh and dwelt among us." God comes to us as a person from a small town. "Okay," Nathaniel says, "we'll follow, Phillip and I. Pleased to be asked." But what about the cross? What about Jesus' suffering and death? What about their own eventual suffering and death? What about following then and there?

In every ordination liturgy in the Book of Common Prayer, there is a question about call. For deacons and priests, it is, "Do you believe that you are truly called by God and his church?" For bishops it is, "Are you *persuaded* that God has called you to the office of bishop?"

But not unlike the Samuel story, not everything is revealed in the call or in the assent to the call. Did I know, for example, that my call to priesthood would involve fixing (or rather, trying to fix) the boiler in the parish house where homeless men showered daily, or hanging out with drug dealers in the pouring rain?

We just ordained Kevin Brown to be our bishop in Delaware. It's an exciting time—a new bishop, a young bishop with lots of energy and ideas. A gifted person who is "persuaded" he is called to the office of bishop. Every bishop soon encounters problems in congregations and problems with clergy. Sometimes very difficult problems. Bishops are often expected to have the wisdom of Solomon, and not unlike other public figures, they can become the focus of praise or blame.

Interestingly, the word "call" does not appear in the service of baptism, even though we call the laos, the laity, the first order of ministry. I wonder if call shouldn't be added to the baptismal service. Why are only ordained people "called"?

When I was going through "the process" eons ago, I was asked if I were called and how would I describe my call? Truthfully, I had no idea how to put that into words. I just knew. But I also knew that that might not be a good enough answer. If I'd have known a little more about quantum physics, I might have had a better answer. Niels Bohr, one of the most famous quantum physicists, once said, "We must be clear, when it comes to atoms, language can only be used as in poetry."

Just like in theology, in talking about God, call, and such, language begins to fail, to reach its limits. Werner Heisenberg, the originator of the "uncertainty principle," once said, "The common division of the world into subject and object, inner world and outer world, body and soul, is no longer adequate." Heisenberg could have been talking about communion.

But I do know one place to go where there is a language about God, about call, that applies to all of us. It is really the language of intimacy, where words don't seem to fail. Psalm 139, not surprisingly, since the spirit is always at work even in the lectionary, is our psalm for today. This is the language of knowing in the deepest sense, and it encompasses all its aspects. It is more than the language of call—it is the language of sustenance. Psalm 139 sings about the relationship that undergirds all our calls.

On the cover of the invitation to my ordination to the priesthood there was a verse from Psalm 139 not cited in today's portion. It read, "Whither can I flee from thy spirit?" So that, fixing the boiler (or trying to fix it) or sitting outside in the pouring rain with the drug dealers, I was in God's presence. There is nowhere to flee God's presence.

I received an email recently from someone suffering a very debilitating disease—one that might make many of us very depressed. Yet she wrote me that she has surrendered to it and even there finds the presence of God.

I hope Samuel and Nathaniel knew Psalm 139. I hope that you do too. I hope that you will learn it by heart. The knowledge it sings about emphasizes both faith and following. This kind of intimacy with God allows us to surrender even in the most difficult circumstances.

The Grace to Begin Again

Beware, keep alert; for you do not
know when the time will come.
Mark 13:33

THE BENEDICTINES BELIEVE AND PRAY ALWAYS FOR THE GRACE to begin again. It is an essential part of their spiritual practice. Today we also begin again. It is the first Sunday in the season of Advent, the first Sunday of the church's new year. We begin again.

In essence, our church year is our corporate spiritual journey, our opportunity to hear the story of God's saving embrace that lets us know that no matter who we are, no matter what we have done, God's welcome is wide enough to encircle us. All of us. We are continually given the grace to begin again and to go deeper, to become what we already are—beloved in God's eyes, precious in God's sight.

But how are we to go on this spiritual journey known as the church year? There is no map because it is not a linear journey from point A to point B, and this journey is mostly about learning to walk in the dark. Meaning, to walk by faith. It's often not a journey of triumph as in the old bumper sticker that read, "I Found It." More often, it is a journey of loss, loss of illusion about ourselves, our powers, our knowledge, our goodness, our self-importance. And it is equally a loss of our notions about God, about where and how God is to be found. Giving up the image of God as the all-powerful white bearded man in the sky is often hard to do. Because God is more often found where we least expect—in the cracks, in our weakness and vulnerability, in our failures, in the grace to begin again. We are approaching the season that proclaims that God came to us as a human being. And we all know how difficult that can be.

But while there is no map, and while God's grace will always trump any of our efforts, I believe that there are qualities of presence, gifts of presence, that we can deepen. I call them qualities of presence because I believe they partake of Presence (with a capital P) itself. That they are being itself as in *yahweh*, I Am, God's very self.

The gospels we hear in this short season of advent, I believe, name those qualities of presence. And I would also say that as we begin a new church year, this corporate spiritual journey, our task is to deepen them.

This morning, Mark's gospel urges us with vivid imagery to stay awake, to watch, to be on high alert for Christ's coming. The earliest church believed that Jesus' return would be soon. But while apocalyptic writing such as Mark's makes for a wild ride, perhaps God is subtler, simpler, more ordinary. Perhaps we miss the presence of God because we haven't learned how to pay attention, perhaps because we are looking for the big AHA, for God to shout in the loudest voice, "HERE I AM, DUDE!"

Simone Weil, the French Resistance fighter during World War II, defined prayer as "paying attention." Poets are good at paying attention, especially to the ordinary. Annie Dillard, in her book Pilgrim at Tinker Creek, writes that it is all "a matter of keeping my eyes open." She describes how she is always on the lookout for the tiny things, the minutiae of larvae hanging from trees, the deer hidden in shadows, that illusive green light that streaks from the sun just at the moment of its setting. In her book, she details the hours she spends seeking what is well-hidden, much like those puzzles in children's magazines that show a tree trunk and ask the reader to find a top, a boot, a parrot, a candle. Things that are in front of us stay hidden until we learn how to see.

The second Sunday in Advent, in our corporate spiritual journey always with the grace to begin again, asks us through the voice of John the Baptist to become aware, to become aware of our real selves, our real motives, our real intentions to repent. John the Baptist challenges us to dare greatly, to dare to be vulnerable, to be imperfect, to become real. He urges us in the strongest sense to turn away from that which keeps us from being aware and present—our addictions to things, substances, and actions that keep us from awareness of our true selves and the presence of God in our midst.

Awareness leads to John the Baptist's next exhortation in Advent Three's gospel—live passionately, be the voice crying in the wilderness, ask the hard questions. Why do the people of the world's great religions continue to slaughter each other in the name of the same God? Why? What kind of madness is this? Have we not grown any wiser, any kinder, any more compassionate? Why is hatred such a well trod path? Is there another way?

Finally, on Advent Four we see in the most improbable figure, an ordinary country teenage girl, what we, you and I, are called to be. The Greeks called it *theotokos*—God-bearers. This ordinary country teenager said perhaps the most important word on the spiritual journey. Yes. Yes, I will. Yes, let it be with me.

Barbara Brown Taylor says it so well.

You can decide to take part in a plan you did not choose, doing things you did not know how to do for reasons you do not entirely understand. You can take part in a thrilling and dangerous scheme with no script and no guarantees. You can agree to smuggle God into the world in your own body. (Gospel Medicine, p. 153)

Dag Hammarsjköld, former Secretary General of the United Nations, wrote :

I don't know Who—or what—put the question, I don't know when it was put. I don't even remember answering. But at some moment I did answer Yes to Someone—or Something—and from that hour I was certain that existence is meaningful and that, therefore, my life, in self-surrender, had a goal. (*Markings*)

We begin again today. We receive the grace to begin again—the grace to become more awake, aware, and passionate—and the grace to say yes, to become God-bearers.

Awakened

What does it mean to be awakened? Often it is to see the light of a new day, or to open our eyes to hope. Sometimes it is to see a path we hadn't realized was there, or to sense a divine presence we thought was lost to us. Awakening sometimes happens in the midst of grief and questioning, and it opens us to the wide arms of compassion.

Finding God in Uncertain Times

And the word became
flesh and lived among us.
John 1:14

We were warned. Not about the Covid-19 virus. We were warned by the author of John's gospel. We were warned clearly. This gospel is about the word made flesh, as John tells us in chapter one. Real flesh, real people, real thirst, real blindness, real death. This Lenten year's gospels put it to us about the word made flesh, about God in stuff, in people. In a Samaritan woman, in a blind man, in a dead man. Almost every last fleshy, incarnational, radical Jesus action runs through these gospel texts. Jesus talks to and drinks with a woman. Jesus spits on dirt and rubs it in a blind man's eyes. Jesus goes to the tomb of a dead friend. As I always say, "Jesus wasn't killed for no reason."

He was just too fleshy, too incarnational, too in our faces, and that is why Jesus was a problem. The author of John's gospel wants us to know that if we are looking for the presence and action of God, we will always find it in flesh, real flesh. God in the flesh is found in thirst, in yearning, in that outsider woman at the well. God is found in a man's blindness, in suffering, suffering through life without being able to see. God is found in death, in a dead man's tomb, in a body wrapped and stowed away in a tomb. Dead for four days, his sisters lament.

We were warned, as were those early followers of the way who were preparing for baptism. These gospel texts were the outline of their baptism class. They were warned, warned that God would show up in their lives in the most difficult places. They already knew that life was difficult. Synagogues were throwing them out for following that itinerant preacher. Roman authorities were hunting them down for sport, to kill them in games at the coliseum. Life was dangerous. They were warned that baptism, following Jesus, was dangerous in dangerous times. They were warned that God was in the danger, in the flesh. And so, the catechumenal questions asked at their baptism took on life and death meaning.

We have been warned, too. God shows up in the flesh. In our flesh, in these moments. And perhaps it is these very moments that will help us to see what the author of John's gospel so badly wants us to see—the word made flesh and dwelling among us full of grace and truth.

Can we find God in these moments of dread, of great fear, of anxiety? Can we find God in these uncertain times? Can we find God in this present danger, in these very fleshy moments?

I believe we can, and I believe we are. We would never have chosen these moments, but they are now ours.

Most of us have already experienced, even in these few weeks of "social distancing," a kind of community that might be far deeper than what we knew before. We have learned that church is in fact "the people gathered" and not a building. We have learned how much we need each other.

Church is no longer casual, no longer optional. We have learned with Mary of Bethany the one thing necessary—to love God, self, and neighbor. We have learned that God is indeed in our midst—in the word preached, in the sacrament blessed, and in the community gathered.

These are powerful learnings. They will stay with us.

We have learned with the woman at the well that we are indeed thirsty. We yearn for living water, for the presence and action of God in our midst. We have learned with the blind man that we yearn to see. We don't need to know how it happened. The technology of healing is irrelevant. We only know that once we were blind, but now we see, that we see the beauty of God's creation and the beauty of each other.

We are learning that we can come back to life even in the worst of circumstances, that we can become unbound, come back to life even after days of death.

We are the woman at the well. We are the blind man. We are Lazarus. And we are at the table, virtual or not. We were warned and now we know. God is in our midst, in the flesh, even in the worst of circumstances.

As Lent draws to a close, and Holy Week dawns, may you

know and feel the presence of God in the flesh, your flesh. May you be well.

To Be Born Again

*Very truly, I tell you, no one can see the kingdom
of God without being born from above.*
John 3:2

NICODEMUS IS ONE OF MY FAVORITE BIBLICAL CHARACTERS.
He strikes me as the quintessential Episcopalian. He is smart,
and he knows the rules. Everything must be decent and in order.
He has high standing in his community. But in spite of all of
this, his soul longs for something. He doesn't know quite what
it is, but he feels a longing for more. So, he goes to the wisdom
teacher he has heard about—Jesus. He probably has his questions
written out on a legal pad, and so that no one will see him, he
goes by night.

But when he meets Jesus, he isn't even able to ask his questions.
Jesus confronts him with, "I tell you no one can see the kingdom
of God without being born again."

"Born again," Nicodemus thinks. "I didn't come here for that.
What does this Jesus mean by that? Clearly my 75-year-old mother
isn't doing *that* again!"

But Jesus persists. "No one can enter the kingdom of God without being born of water and spirit." Sensing Nicodemus' confusion, he says, "Do not be astonished that I said you must be born from above. The wind blows where it will, and you hear the sound of it, but you do not know where it comes from or where it goes."

"As if that helps," Nicodemus laments.

So, what do we make of being born again, being born from above, being born from the womb of God? Being born of water and spirit?

This is a key Lenten question because this year's gospels that we are hearing are the outline of the ancient catechumenates' preparation for baptism in the earliest church.

None of us got to choose our biological births. We just got here. Our parents conceived us, and here we are. When I think about my own conception, made from fifty percent William Pinkney Gill and fifty percent Eleanor Coleman Gill, it's quite a combination. The best way to describe my birth parents is from a photograph. My parents are standing together. My mother is wearing a simple, tasteful, attractive dress, and my father has on bib jeans, a flannel shirt, and white tennis shoes. They indeed married their opposites, and I have been sorting that out my entire life. And, actually, according to John's Jesus, we don't get to choose being born again! Jesus says later in John's gospel, "You did not choose me. I chose you." So perhaps Nicodemus was already chosen and didn't know it... yet.

But what does it mean to be born again? To be born from the womb of God? To be born of water and spirit? If God gives birth to us, what does that look like? References to God birthing us are all over scripture. Think of Psalm 139. "Before I formed you in the womb, I knew you." In Hebrew, the word womb translates as compassion. To be born of God, from God's womb, is to be born from compassion. To be born of water and spirit is to be born of the force that hovered over the chaos and created the universe. Very powerful, indeed!

If we look back a few Sundays to the story of Jesus' baptism, we know that Jesus got in that water and heard the spirit name him beloved. "You are my beloved" (Matthew 3:17). And everyone else in the River Jordan heard the same thing. The spirit voice was spread over the waters. "You are my beloved. With you I am well pleased."

This is exactly what Nicodemus longs for—to be born of a compassionate spirit that names him as beloved. All the knowledge of the law that Nicodemus has will not save him, will not heal him, will not make him whole. But being born of water and spirit will.

How does it happen? It's as mysterious as the wind. We can feel it. We can see its effect. But it remains a mystery, a grace that cannot be tamed.

I pray that each of us will be born again, and again, and again.

You Have Nothing to Fear

He answered, "I do not know
whether he is a sinner. One thing I
do know. That though I was blind,
now I see.
John 9:25

"One thing I do know, that though I was blind, now I see." That's exactly what the blind man knows. He cannot explain this miraculous healing. He simply knows that it happened.

Isn't that often the way with healing? We know it has happened. We have experienced it. But for many reasons, we often have difficulty saying how it happened. There are many reasons. Healing—deep, true, saving—often defies explanation. It doesn't fit into neat, scientific, verifiable categories. Sometimes it is even beyond prosaic language itself. The 18th century Anglican priest and hymnodist William Cowper, who suffered terribly from depression, wrote hymn texts as a kind of therapy, and in the process experienced profound healing. The text of one of his hymns begins, "God moves in a mysterious way his wonders to perform/ He plants his footsteps in the sea, and rides upon the storm."

You have heard my healing story many times—so many that some of you can quote it. That's not just a bad thing, is it? In fact, someone quoted my story to me the other night and got it right! But in case you forgot, or have never heard it, in the midst of chemotherapy for breast cancer when I was acutely aware that I could die, I was addressed with these words: "Carlyle, you have nothing to fear in life or in death." That one sentence changed my life. I couldn't tell you exactly which member of the trinity addressed me. I only knew it was true. I had been afraid of living, and I was resolved to live with all my heart.

A neurologist and self-described skeptic had a similar experience. In the midst of a deadly illness, he had an awareness of healing. He said, "To take one more shot at putting it into words, it would run something like this: you are loved and cherished. You have nothing to fear. There is nothing you can do wrong. If I had to boil it down further, it would be, simply, love." The difficult part for this neurologist was telling his physician colleagues, just like the blind man in our gospel story.

Some of us have healing experiences that are not in the midst of life or death situations but are just as powerful. The other evening someone was talking to me about coming to St. Peter's. "I had no idea there was more than the rules. I had no idea about grace. That God loved me. Me, of all people!" That is healing.

Some of us are still waiting. Many of us are living with pain of all kinds. Some of us are walking by faith alone. I am reminded of a Jesuit's words. "It is often the night in which the Lord appears, not always as felt reassurance, but as the power to continue faithful, even when faithfulness means simply putting one foot in front of the other."

The organist and choir director at St. Alban's who introduced me to William Cowper says, "The eyes opened by faith and trust will be able to see the blessings in this life." A trusting heart can understand what cannot be seen, he seems to tell us. Cowper channeled his tortured mind to craft poetry. For his sake I wish he could have created without suffering. But God's ways are mysterious and I will take Cowper's words to heart and simply trust in God's mysterious ways.

We don't know how healing happens. It is truly a part of God's mysterious way, but we do know from the healing of the blind man that God takes the dirt, the mud, the places, the materials we least expect in our lives and makes a paste, an opportunity for healing, for new creation.

By the end of today's gospel story, the blind man's inner eyes are opened. He sees, he knows the author of his healing, God's very presence in his life.

And so we pray that our eyes will open to see God's presence in the world about us and in the world within us.

Dashed Hopes

Now on that same day, two of them
were going to a village, called Emmaus,
about seven miles from Jerusalem, and
talking with each other about all these
things that had happened.
Luke 24:13

WHAT I REALLY LIKE BEST ABOUT THE BIBLICAL STORIES IS their honesty and humor. These qualities are embedded in today's gospel text—Luke's story of the road to Emmaus. There is much humor here, like Cleopas and company saying to the stranger, the risen Christ, "So, dude, are you the only one who doesn't know what just happened in Jerusalem? Dude!" However, I think honesty wins the day in this story, because each of us is on this same road to Emmaus.

Honesty. While our culture would like the season of Easter to be in yellows and other pastel colors with bunnies and flowers, the biblical story is utterly honest about people's reactions to Jesus' resurrection. The second Sunday after Easter is about doubt. "No," Thomas says. "I will not believe unless I can put my hands on the man." Doubt matters a lot. Doubt is engagement because under doubt is the yearning to be in real relationship. And Thomas is the first to say, "My Lord and my God." This marks a real relationship as a result of his doubt. The season of Easter, these fifty days, is a time to engage our doubts, to see where they lead, to see if we too can be in honest relationship with God.

Our lives, yours and mine, are full of dashed hopes. Each of us is on a road to Emmaus. We had hoped that the cancer would not come back. We had hoped that there would be a final cure instead of putting up with this noxious treatment. We had hoped that the parent, the friend, the partner of many years, would not die. We had hoped our children and our grandchildren would be well and thrive. We did not want to be on this road of grief and disappointment. Yet, true to this biblical story and true to our lives, it is only with a broken heart, an open heart, a grieving heart, a disappointed heart, that we have the possibility of knowing the stranger who walks with us, who in unexpected moments—perhaps at the moment of receiving bread and wine—warms our hearts, gives us the knowledge that no matter what, we are not alone.

At the heart of incarnation is the sure knowing that God as person has traveled this road and knows physical suffering, grief, and loss, even the abandonment of God. Therefore, as risen presence, he is never a stranger to our suffering, to our Emmaus roads. We do not travel alone because our guest, the one who travels with us, is also our host. Been there, been on this road.

And therefore, we ask, perhaps we beg, "Be known to us in the breaking of the bread." And the answer from the one who walks with us on this road is, "Fear not, I am with you." And his words continue as the words in the great hymn, "How Firm a Foundation."

> When through the deep waters I call thee to go,
> The rivers of woe shall not thee overflow;
> For I will be with thee thy troubles to bless,
> And sanctify to thee thy deepest distress. (The Hymnal 1982, p. 637)

I, too, am on the road to Emmaus, and I know this is so.

Sin and Forgiveness

*John said to the crowds that came
out to be baptized by him, "You
brood of vipers! Who warned you to
flee from the wrath to come?"*
Luke 3:7

ADVENT IS A PECULIAR SEASON. IT MARKS THE BEGINNING OF the church year at the end of the chronological year. There are strange themes like the end of the world, and strange characters like John the Baptist. The season of Advent has the possibility of being an intensely spiritual time, yet it is set squarely in the midst of immense pressure to get out and spend lots of money. So, Advent is an odd time and very easy to miss. If all we need is a new pair of socks or a good book, Advent is really irrelevant. But if we need a savior, then it's a different matter.

You see, Christmas only really makes sense if we have some awareness—however dim—that we need something. Some*one*, actually. In our culture, coming across our true need is often difficult because there is so much we can buy that will plug those holes, at least for a short time. But this sermon is not a rant about consumerism. In fact, that's too simple. I want to look closely at what the season of Advent might help us uncover, perhaps even our real need for a savior.

The Advent odd man, John the Baptist, can help us. He points to one of the biggest issues in all of our lives— forgiveness. He's the one who troubles our waters and stirs up this topic. He's the one who comes through our various wildernesses waving this issue in front of us.

Many years ago, when I was at St. Alban's parish in Washington, D.C., it was my charge and delight to organize adult forums. I had preached a sermon on forgiveness that stirred a lot of conversation, so we offered a four-part adult forum series on the topic. It was the most heavily attended series we ever had, to the point of standing room only in a very large parish hall. It was a topic that clearly struck a nerve.

But as good as that series was, there is really no better introduction to the topic of forgiveness than the actual experience of screwing up. Badly. Or to put it in theological language that no one likes to hear—it's about sin. I don't mean just eating too much chocolate. I mean doing something that hurts another person so badly that there is nothing we can do to fix it.

Often when we talk about forgiveness, we talk about how to forgive another person for something she has done to us. And that's not easy. But as hard as forgiving another can be, it still puts us in a power position—we are the ones who can grant forgiveness or not.

We can decide when or if to forgive. We can decide if the other is worthy of our forgiveness.

But standing in need of forgiveness is another matter. It is most assuredly not a power position, and if we have wronged another and long for forgiveness, we have no control over whether we actually receive it or not. Longing for forgiveness, needing forgiveness, is like being naked with no place to hide. We have screwed up. Someone else has seen it. We can feel ashamed and guilty, but none of those feelings can cover us or do anything to repair the broken relationship. Only forgiveness will clothe our nakedness.

It's no wonder that the root meaning of forgiveness in Hebrew means to cover—to recover. We have all been there. Some of us are there. Think about the times when you have really screwed up, really hurt someone, and there's nothing you could do to fix it. It's one of the most helpless places to be. It is embarrassing because we have to acknowledge that we did something wrong and that we aren't perfect. There's no undoing it, no making it better, no glossing over it. Our action might even mean the end of a relationship with someone very important to us. In fact, the root meaning of the word *sin*—a word fallen out of favor in 21st century liberal American vocabulary—is separation, loss of relationship with God, self, and neighbor.

This separation from God, self, and neighbor is the reality, the human situation, the sin, that John the Baptist points to in this morning's gospel. It is manifest not only in our individual relationships but in our corporate life. Think for a minute about our environment. The biblical story tells us that we were given the earth as a gift, that we are stewards. We have failed miserably. Global warming threatens the entire planet. The biblical story tells us that we were given each other for companionship. We have failed miserably. War is our well-worn conflict resolution strategy.

I say all of this, joining with that odd Advent man John the Baptist, not to make anyone feel bad, or guilty, or ashamed. Feeling bad makes us impotent. Feeling guilty gives us the illusion that we are doing something when we're not. Shame only paralyzes us.

The honest recognition of our sinfulness and our need for forgiveness—whether on an individual or corporate level—brings us to the heart of Advent. In his Advent poem, "For the Time Being," W.H. Auden put it this way: "We who must die demand a savior." Or, in my words, "If all we need is a pair of socks and a good book, Advent is not for us." If we don't know deep in our bones our desperate need for forgiveness, then the Tanger Outlets will be a fine substitute.

The gospel of Luke is our companion for the new church year that began last Sunday. Luke's gospel is the compassion gospel. Story after story after story in Luke's gospel is about the reality of God's forgiving love for all sorts and conditions of people. From the prodigal son who squanders everything recklessly, bottoms out and returns home to the waiting and open arms of a loving father, to the woman who crashed Simon the Pharisee's dinner party bursting with her immense gratitude for the forgiveness she knows she has received from Jesus, Luke describes for us the essential quality of God made flesh, made visible, made concrete in Jesus of Nazareth.

This grace, this outrageous grace of forgiveness to all of us who don't deserve it, is the very heart of God because God *chooses* to forgive, to be in relationship with us no matter what. It is the yearning of God. Forgiveness is a costly grace as we learn in Holy Week, but a gift nonetheless, for each one of us. This Godly grace of forgiveness may not immediately repair our broken relationships, but it is what St. Benedict described when he said, "Always we begin again."

Unpacking

CAROL TELLS A WONDERFUL STORY FROM HER YEARS WORKING for the Peace Corps in Nepal. She wanted to go on a trek, of course. Nepal is home to some of the most beautiful mountains in the world. So, she set out on her trek, her journey to those mountains, or at least for a better view of them. But she realized that her view of the beautiful vistas was obscured, not by weather, but by weight. Her backpack was so heavy that she was bent over and could only see the ground beneath her feet. Not until she let go of that heavy pack, until she allowed someone else to carry it, could she look up and see the beauty of Everest.

Most of us don't have to go to Nepal to have that experience. I am a notorious over-packer, whether for a weekend trip or a two-week retreat. While packing, I think, "It's probably best to have more than two turtlenecks. You never know when you might need an extra." Or socks. I love to pack lots of socks. You never know when…And like Carol's backpack in Nepal, my suitcase is always very heavy.

The season of Lent that we begin today is often described as a journey, a journey into the heart of God, not unlike a trek to a beautiful majestic mountain. And one might say that the spiritual practice prescribed for this journey could simply be called "unpacking." Most of us carry around a lot of stuff, not too many turtlenecks or socks, but other weightier things that are harder to let go. Things we've been carrying for years.

Things like our need to control the world, to make things turn out the way we want them to, to make people behave the way we think they should. That's pretty heavy and can be quite burdensome.

Some of us have a rather large collection of "shoulds" and "oughts" coupled with an equally large collection of "onlys." If only I had done that or not done this. Regrets. They are heavy too.

Tucked into some luggage we've been carrying for years and permeating our entire suitcase, is our fear of our own humanity, our vulnerability, our weaknesses, our inability to do and be as we would like. This fear, known as shame, can be one of the heaviest things we carry.

These are only a few. There is much more. Our view that we are right, absolutely right. Our fear of those different from us. Our fear of death.

Whatever we carry weighs us down. It keeps us from seeing

the mountain, the beauty, the presence of God in the present moment, and from really seeing each other. So how shall we engage in this Lenten practice of unpacking?

Jesus throws us a hint in the Ash Wednesday gospel. "Beware of practicing your piety before others." In other words, piety is not the answer. It's just a cover-up for all of those things that have been weighing us down. Piety only increases our load.

When Carol was trekking in Nepal, the only way she was finally able to see that mountain's majesty was to give away her backpack and let someone else carry it for her. Perhaps our Lenten journey into the presence of God begins with letting go, with trusting that God can carry our baggage. That's a lot of trust, I know, but even the act of trust can lighten our load. Rather than be vague, I want to suggest a Lenten-lightening-the-load practice.

Whenever you notice one of those weighty items in your spiritual suitcase (and you will because they pop up daily if not hourly!), simply notice it. Don't judge it—that's added weight! There it is. Then simply say, "I let it go, with God's help."

I don't promise immediate results, but I do know that over time, with God's help, our baggage and our burdens will lighten.

I wish you a holy and light Lent.

I am Seen, Known, Open to God

*Many Samaritans from that city
believed in him because of the
woman's testimony, "He told me
everything I have ever done."*
John 4:39

You have heard me say that this year's Lent gospels are.... just the best. They provide a wonderful outline of the spiritual journey, a faith journey, not in a linear fashion but in a human, tender complex way that is very much how you and I are today. When we say "faith," we mean it as the biblical story understands it. Not a set of beliefs, but a relationship. Actually, I believe the entire biblical story is a narrative of this journey, filled with real people with real lives who are not perfect and are touched and changed by the presence of God. You and I are here this morning because we are on the same journey.

The Year A Lent texts from the Gospel of John are all about people on this journey. Last Sunday we heard about Nicodemus (we called him "Nick at night"), a man like so many of us. A man with standing in the community, inquiring but not wanting to go too deeply so as to be unseemly. Wanting to know a little about Jesus, but not too much. And just a bit, well, ashamed of his inquiry because he thinks he should know everything or at least appear to know everything. So he goes to Jesus by night to inquire. And he is left dumbfounded with talk of being born again, of the spirit that blows where it will. I am sure he was very disappointed, if not totally confused. But we know that ultimately he went deeper, engaged Jesus deeper, because he was at the tomb with spices to anoint Jesus' body. Only someone close would do that.

The woman at the well is a very different person. The contrast between her and Nicodemus is night and day, especially as she meets Jesus at the well at the brightest part of the day—noon. She has no standing in the community. She is a woman. She is a Samaritan and therefore shunned by the Jews. She is not even named in the text. She is simply engaged in the tasks of daily living—going to the well to bring water back to her community. She is a water bearer. That's what women did then. She is very vulnerable, unprotected with no husband. It is amazing, or maybe not, given our prejudices, that she is often viewed as a sinner when that word is never mentioned in the text. She is divorced because *men left her*. She has been left a lot. And the relationship she now has leaves her very defenseless without the legal protection of marriage.

Jewish theologian Martin Buber once said, "All real living is meeting." The encounter of Jesus with the woman at the well is about a real meeting. One might say that about the spiritual journey, about the faith journey. It is about meeting, and therefore about really living.

She meets Jesus at the well. Jesus begins the conversation by asking for water because he is thirsty after a long journey. The conversation begins with need—with Jesus' need. Jesus opens with his vulnerability, with his thirst. The woman is taken aback. We see her in the moment surprised that a man, a rabbi, a Jew, would ask something of *her*, a nobody, a Samaritan, a woman. In this moment we see that real meeting is now possible. Both Jesus and the woman are open to each other.

Jesus then does a remarkable thing, a very compassionate thing. Yes, he's known for that, but still it is remarkable, and even more so for us today. He sees her. He sees her vulnerability, that she has been left five times and lives insecurely now. He sees her and her real situation, who she really is. He sees the shame she carries as a Samaritan, as a divorced woman. It isn't often that we are really seen and engaged for who we really are. But Jesus does. He does not judge her. He simply lets her understand that she is known. That is a real gift—to be seen and known. She learns something she has never experienced before—that she is worthy and valued. Known.

This is a real conversation, a real meeting. The woman at the well is then emboldened to ask a question. Where should she worship, where should she find this living water? This was not a trivial question like should I go to St. Peter's or All Saints, but a powerful question because it is what had divided Jews and

Samaritans for centuries. Her question is a genuine faith journey question—where, how can I meet, be in relationship with the living God? How can I sustain that relationship?

Jesus gives her a very surprising, and perhaps to some religious people, a heretical answer. Not in the usual places, not in the pious places, but in spirit and in truth. In other words, just as you are, just where you are. He tells her that for her, a vulnerable woman performing the tasks of daily living, being open is enough. And then she learns the depth of Jesus' answer. In this very open and very vulnerable encounter, she has met the living God. I am. Being. Presence. Essence. Yahweh. However we name it.

And because she has been seen and known and loved, maybe for the first time in her life, she can take risks. She runs back to her community to tell them all about her encounter with Jesus at the well. Perhaps *she* is the first evangelist because she is bearing good news, saving news, *living* water. A very different, transformed water bearer.

This sermon could end right here, but I want to be sure that you see the pattern in this woman's journey, because it is ours too. She is living an ordinary life, performing the tasks of daily living. Aren't we all? And she is willing to be open, to be vulnerable with this stranger, since he too is willing to be the same with her. This stranger sees her as no one else ever has. She is known deeply and she learns that she is a person of worth in the knowing. She learns that the faith journey is not about correctness or correct place but about oneness, about allowing, about spirit and truth.

And she is changed.

May this be true, and may this be given to you and to me.

Images

*Do you want me to release for you
the King of the Jews?*
John 18:39

WE ARE, ALL OF US, AWASH IN IMAGES. IMAGES FROM HOLLY-wood, images from Madison Avenue. We live in a virtual soup of imagery that tells us how to look, how to feel, how to behave, how to be successful, what is important, and what will make us look important. Women know that being thin is paramount, that being young is extremely important. Men know that being well-built and virile is important. We are, however, not all thin, young, muscular, or virile. But the images of what we are ideally supposed to be are never far from our awareness.

One of the best ways to understand the power of images is to think of our self-images. They are usually formed very early in our childhoods and are very hard to shake, even when the actual data about ourselves contradicts these early formed images. Think for a moment about what you were told about yourself when you were a child and how it shaped your lasting self-image.

Our images of God are just as powerful as our Hollywood and Madison Avenue images of bodily perfection and our early formed self-images. Most of us were raised with the old white man in the sky image of God who was usually unhappy with us. Images of Jesus haven't fared any better. Jesus is most often portrayed as a young white man—not quite as unhappy—but often rather vapid, bordering on wimpy.

I mention all of this because today we celebrate the last Sunday in a long season of Pentecost with the feast of Christ the King. I think it's really weird, frankly, since Jesus did everything he possibly could to dissuade people from the notion that he was a king, that he was the powerful one who would get rid of the Romans and restore Israel to the golden years of King David. Even his closest associates didn't get it. Remember the story of Peter, how he found it so incredulous that Jesus of all people would suffer and die? And Jesus' response to Peter—"Get behind me, Satan!" (Matthew 16:23). Strong words.

But Christ the King? An actual Sunday called that? We have company at our house for the Thanksgiving weekend. I told them I was preaching this Sunday and that it was Christ the King Sunday. They wanted to know where that came from, so like a good 21st century preacher, I googled it. I found an article that told me that in 1925 Pope Pius XI established this Sunday as a way of countering secularism, proclaiming that Christ was king over all, secular society as well as governments of all kinds. And the picture that was embedded in the article was amazing. There is

Jesus—looking white, young, mild, bland, dressed in kingly robes with an orb and scepter as well as a crown floating just above his head. Frankly, it's a ridiculous image. If anything, an image such as this only shows us how irrelevant Christianity is today. Black Friday continues on as usual. Secularism is alive and well. Governments are in just as much trouble as ever.

But if we look at the actual images embedded in scripture, another picture, another person, another reality emerges. In today's gospel, Jesus is on trial. Pilate, the Roman government's authority in Palestine, wants to know if Jesus is the king of the Jews. Is Jesus planning to overthrow Roman rule and thus be tried for treason and sedition? Just what kind of king is this Jew, Pilate wants to know.

The telling image to Pilate's question is the image of Jesus painted in the gospels at the Crucifixion. Jesus is stripped of his clothes, robed in a purple cloak with a crown of thorns hung on his head. "There!" they said. "There is the king of the Jews!" There is the king. Naked, shamed, shunned, defenseless, dying, weak, utterly vulnerable. That is the king.

The night before I was ordained to the priesthood, I read an article that has stayed close to me for the last thirty-six years and has made more sense the older I've become. The author of the article begins by saying that in most professions the question that is asked is, "Is this person strong enough to be a doctor, lawyer, teacher…?" But the author goes on to say that the question to be asked of priesthood is of its essence the opposite. "Is this person weak enough to be a priest?" By weakness he doesn't mean sin, but he defines weakness as "the experience of a peculiar liability to suffering… which issues in the inability to secure our own future, to protect ourselves from any adversity." The author says this is exactly the Jesus described in the epistle to the Hebrews: "One who was tempted in every way as we are… who can sympathize with our weakness since he himself is beset with weakness."

This Jesus is not a powerful king or even a mild-mannered bland king living way up in the sky with a crown floating just above his head. This is a person who lived and loved hard, deeply, truly, who practiced self-emptying, who embraced his humanity and therefore his vulnerability, who endured great suffering, who died a painful and humiliating death. Who was weak.

This Jesus is Emmanuel—God with us, God with us where we actually are—weak, vulnerable, human. As the author of my article says, "It is the night in which the Lord appears. Not always felt reassurance but as the power to continue faithful even when faithfulness means simply putting one foot in front of the other." This Jesus is way, way better and way more capable of actually saving us than a king. This Jesus knows what it's like to be one of us, and this Jesus knows what image matters most. Not the young and thin image or the muscular and virile image of our often-misinformed self-images, but the image of God, in which each of us is created. Knowing that, knowing that we are created in God's image and therefore precious in God's sight, gives us the freedom to be and to become our true selves—human with the gift and grace of being.

I leave you with a few questions to ponder from David Lose in a blogpost on "In the Meantime" in 2012.

Can we allow our images of God to conform to the vulnerability we see in Jesus? Can we imagine that to be a follower of Jesus is to embrace vulnerability rather than to use our faith to defend ourselves against it? Can we imagine that church isn't the place you go when you've got it all figured out but instead where you go to gather with others on the way?

The Grace of Ordinary Time

THERE ARE MANY HOMILETICAL OPPORTUNITIES IN TODAY'S gospel. All worthy themes. But I am not preaching on any of them. My text for this sermon is TODAY—the first Sunday in ordinary time and the texts of our lives.

After all the liturgical high drama of Holy Week, Easter, Pentecost, and Trinity Sunday, we come today to what the liturgical calendar calls the first Sunday in ordinary time. Liturgically, ordinary time stretches from today to the first Sunday of Advent. Ordinary time is the longest season of the church year. It's well… ordinary. No big feasts, no gnashing of teeth, no breast beating, no waiting, no loud alleluias, no rejoicing. Nothing special. Just ordinary time. Ordinary as in simply living our lives, getting through the day, putting one foot in front of the other.

Actually, that's enough for me. But it's not easy in our culture. If the news media is to be believed—and most of us believe it if not thrive on it—crises are the order of the day. Ordinariness does not sell newspapers or increase the number of viewers who will buy whatever is advertised and therefore keep the news media in business. Think about how the advertising industry shapes our thinking. It doesn't care for ordinariness either. We are bombarded with what is missing from our lives, what we need to make us happy, feel better, look younger, and be more potent. God forbid we should appreciate the ordinary, the everyday, the actuality of our lives.

But truly, I would take ordinary time any day. My ordinary day begins with a fabulous cup of coffee sipped slowly while I watch the ordinary activity on the wetlands of Lewes Beach, while I listen to the sounds of the mockingbirds, red-winged blackbirds, cardinals, robins, and a host of others I can't name. One day I saw an osprey perched in a dead tree munching on a fish that was almost bigger than he (or she). Actually, watching all of this ordinariness brings tears to my eyes. It makes me think of Simone Weil's definition of prayer. "Prayer is paying attention." And it makes me think of the poet Mary Oliver who thrives on the ordinariness of Cape Cod. She said once about her writing, "I am sensual in order to be spiritual."

Yet most of us 21st century skeptics are waiting for the big spiritual moment, the "aha" that will finally prove once and for all that there is a God. This God will lift us out of the ordinariness of our lives and fix what Madison Avenue seems unable to cure. But God seems to operate in exactly the opposite way. This long liturgical season called ordinary time is about people like you and I trying to live our lives as best we can—putting one foot in front of the other, struggling with pain, disease, loss, rejection, difficult family members, poverty, and a host of other things. And this long liturgical season called ordinary time is about the God, the incarnate presence of God, who meets them and us precisely there, in our ordinariness.

I am reminded of Jesus' question in the Gospel story we will hear two weeks from today—the story of the woman who crashed Simon the Pharisee's dinner party. "Do you see this woman?" What a great question. Do we actually see what is right in front of us? What is inside of us? What is right next to us? Who is right next to us for that matter? Do we see the ordinary? Do we love it?

This is what we need to pray for—sight, the gift of paying attention, even to the hard things in our lives. The tradition to which we belong tells us over and over and over again that this, the ordinariness of our lives, is where God is to be found.

This week a small group will gather with a woman who is dying of pancreatic cancer. She has chosen to gather her closest friends to say good-bye, to say thank you for all the ordinary moments in her life. She herself would wish for only one thing—more ordinary time. I leave you with this quote by the poet Mark Nepo.

The further I wake into this life, the more I realize that God is everywhere and the extraordinary is waiting quietly beneath the skin of all that is ordinary....God is under the porch as well as on top of the mountain and this joy is in both the front row and the bleachers.

Grief and Gratitude

SOMEONE ONCE WROTE, "GRIEF AND GRATITUDE ARE KINDRED souls, each pointing to the beauty of what is transient and given to us by grace."

If anyone knew that truth, it was Mary Pitts Helms. In the last four years, Mary came to know those kindred souls of grief and gratitude acutely. She simultaneously lost her voice and found her voice. In her grief, as she was diagnosed and struggled with Bulbar ALS, she marveled at the wonders many of us take for granted and which she took for granted and lost. Her life, her children, her grandchildren, her partner, and her friends became exquisitely more precious. She knew deeply the transience of life as well as life's wondrous and simple graces. She learned how to speak of them all in a different voice—a poet's voice. In the introduction to her first book of poetry, *Lost and Found*, she wrote this:

If I made a list years ago of 100 things in my future, ALS would not have made the list, but the list would have been made with the assumption of a loving God who has good things in store for me. I am still guided by that faith, believing that all circumstances contain gifts. I want to recognize and receive them. That is not an easy task at times, and the process often involves deep grief as well as joy.

Mary knew, as only Mary could know, the grace, as she says, that "all circumstances contain gifts." She knew that even in a disease as devastating as Bulbar ALS, there were gifts. Her poem, "Pride," from her first book of poetry, *Lost and Found* (p. 3), speaks of these hidden gifts.

I know now I loved my voice more than God.
I loved my speaking more than silence,
my pronouncements more than obedience.
I had no grain of humility living in my field of pride.
My slowness in discerning the meaning
in languages other than my own limited one
was my stubborn ear to the pain of others,
the weary travelers who had no place to rest,
the childless women who wept in secret,
the men who scurried in fear of losing their place
in the nameless line of slaves to work,
the children without a home.
So seduced by my own song,

I could not hear theirs in a minor key.

Now a mute exultation of knowing,

free of my own design,

convicted and forgiven

embraced in holy arms.

Suffering may be the only road to compassion and to humility. It is so easy to say and so hard to live. Mary Helms lived it.

And she lived a rich, full, and joy-filled life. She loved her family—her four children, her sisters, her parents, her devoted partner George. She loved the beach. She gave generously of herself. I never drive by Epworth United Methodist Church without thinking of Mary and how she loved working on the building and raising the funds for it. We live near the Children's Beach House and think of her there. She had many careers before moving here permanently, some I've only recently known about. She helped shape so many lives through her coaching practice. She and George gathered many around the work of Thomas Merton. She was very encouraging to me. When I told her that I was hesitant to follow the urging of a fellow St. Peter's parishioner to publish a book of my sermons, she said, without skipping a beat, "It's your legacy, Carlyle! Do it!" So I borrowed her editor, and when that book is published, it will be dedicated to Mary.

Jesus was Mary's kin. Jesus also knew grief and gratitude. The gospel story we heard about the death of Lazarus was chosen by Mary for this service. Jesus was deeply grieved by Lazarus' death.

At his tomb, Jesus wept. And Jesus always knew that gratitude was at the heart of God's abiding presence. It was Jesus' intention that we know joy and know it abundantly.

In her poem, "When Death Comes," Mary Oliver speaks of her desire to live fully in the world and to meet death knowing the richness of that engagement. She expresses her belief that eternity is but another step in life, that life and death are connected with threads of joy. Mary Helms was such a sojourner on this earth, not merely a visitor, but a full participant. And she saw death not as an ending, but a new beginning. Her poem, "Death Light" (*Lost and Found*, p. 20), ends with these words:

> That's what I will do
> as I move to death in the sky,
> shine and shine and shine as if full
> because I will be
> full, more and more,
> of the light.

In gratitude and in grief, Mary knew life's gifts.

Is It True? Do You Trust Me?

Mary Magdalene went and announced
to the disciples, "I have seen the Lord."
John 20:18

WE ARE ALL HERE FOR A VARIETY OF REASONS. SOME OF US ARE here because someone in our family told us to come. Others of us are here because Easter Sunday is a traditional family outing that includes church and brunch. Some of us are here because this is our parish church and we have been through Holy Week and are more than ready for Easter. But it is probably safe to say that all of us are here with the same question. Is it true? Is it really true that Jesus was raised from the dead? What an important and difficult question. Because if it's true, then my life is turned upside down. If it isn't true, my life is turned upside down. What if there really is a God and this God has the power to raise someone from the dead? I'd better straighten up my act!

But maybe we should start with something a little simpler, something we can wrap our minds around, like the historical Jesus. That would be easier. There would be verifiable, independent sources who could tell us that a person named Jesus actually lived and died. Then we could move on to Jesus' teachings. They might be a little perplexing and challenging, but nothing like being raised from the dead.

The truth is, however, that the earliest church, the earliest people gathered around Jesus, began with the resurrection. This was the first story told. We know that each of the gospels began with the Crucifixion/Resurrection narrative, and all the rest was added later. They began with Easter. They began with what is hardest for us, much like our first reading this morning. Good old Peter, the guy who claimed he didn't know the man, who was scared out of his mind, is the one with the resurrection sermon! The chief doubter, the chief denier, is the first preacher!

So, if the church began with, is actually founded on the Resurrection, and we're not certain it's true, then is it possible that the church has been a lie these thousands of years?

One thing we do know. The biblical story tends to include the whole truth—the good, the bad, and the ugly. If we take the time to read it, we learn that there are many unsavory characters in it—liars, cheaters, stealers, murderers, adulterers, and more. The biblical story tends to tell it all. This is seen clearly in Crucifixion/Resurrection narratives. The disciples, those closest to Jesus, don't look good. They fall asleep. They desert him. They deny that they know him. The male disciples in this morning's gospel story spend most of their time running from one place to the other. Racing back and forth from tomb to town. We can understand that. When important events happen in our lives, there's a lot of nervous running from here to there.

But what is most curious in this morning's Resurrection narrative is that the first person Jesus appears to after his death is Mary Magdalene. Yes, she does a little running around, but compared to the male disciples, she spends more time standing still. Listening. It is she who hears her name, her very presence summoned by someone who knows her well, a presence she recognizes. As one commentator on this story aptly says, "If someone in the first century had wanted to invent a story about people seeing Jesus, they wouldn't have dreamed of giving the star part to a woman, let alone Mary Magdalene."

Well, that's all very interesting, but it doesn't answer our real question—is it true? Is it true that Jesus was actually raised from the dead?

What we need to know while pondering that question are two things. First, we can't know for sure, and Jesus' Resurrection from the dead is something so big, so beyond our ordinary awareness that doubt must be included. Just like all the other really big things in our lives, like love. When someone loves us, really loves us, it's often unbelievable. Loves me? we might ask. We might have just a smidgen of doubt. Or the times when we experience the presence of God out of the blue while watching something exquisitely beautiful or sitting with someone who is dying, or while we experience ourselves being at the end of our rope. Did that really happen? we might ask. Did I make it up? Did

God really come close to me? This Sunday, this feast day of the Resurrection, asks us to swim in a mystery way beyond us. And actually, learning to swim in mystery is not a bad skill because there is so much mystery in our lives.

But most importantly, our inquiry, "Is it true?" begs the question of the meaning of faith. Many of us have faith somehow tied to belief, which means we are able to give intellectual assent to something. But the root meaning of the word faith is actually "trust." Earlier in John's gospel, Jesus asks Martha of Bethany, "Do you believe that I am the Resurrection and the Life?" In other words, Jesus says, "Do you trust me on this?" Trust, then, is about participating in a relationship, an intimate relationship. Without trust, intimate relationships are not possible.

So, perhaps that's Jesus' question to us today. Do you trust me on this?

All I can tell you is that I do, and it has made all the difference.

Spirituality and Cancer: My Own Journey

Summer Spirituality Series

I RECOGNIZE THAT THIS IS A HUGE EMOTIONAL AND SPIRITUAL topic that has affected most people. Whether we ourselves have had cancer or are the parents, partners, relatives, caregivers, or friends, we have all been touched by this disease. As a past and present cancer patient, I am aware of cancer's broad reach. I also believe in the power of story-telling because it gives shape and meaning to our experiences helps us feel less isolated.

Before I tell you my story, I want to present a working/living understanding of spirituality. The word spirit in the Judeo-Christian tradition comes from the Hebrew *ruach*, meaning wind, and *nephesh*, meaning life force. It is translated into the Greek as *pneuma* breath which means spirit. With that linguistic background in mind, I believe that spirituality is involved with life, with living, with being alive, and with the power that animates those states. Spirituality is whatever truly brings us to life, in all senses of that term, and also allows us to go on that sacred journey of our dying.

All of the world's religions offer a spirituality, a way of honoring and coming to life. The Christian path believes that God's spirit, God's life force, is embodied in creation and incarnate in the person of Jesus of Nazareth, and that the Holy Spirit is actively communicating God's very life to us and in us. Barbara Brown Taylor, one of my favorite Episcopal priests, says:

> *Prayer, according to Brother David, is waking up to the presence of God no matter where I am or what I am doing. When I am fully alert to whatever or whoever is right in front of me; when I am electrically aware of the tremendous gift of being alive; when I am able to give myself wholly to the moment I am in, then I am in prayer. Prayer is happening...God is happening, and I am lucky enough to know that I am in The Midst.* (*An Altar in the World: A Geography of Faith*, p. 178)

There are many other paths to coming alive, and Buddhism, in particular, has helped me along one of them.

I want to begin by saying that having cancer, struggling through the treatment for cancer, brought me to life. That is not to say that it was easy—far from it. But I think I'm actually saying that having cancer was a spiritual path for me all on its own and an unexpected gift as well.

In 1993, I was 47 and in my sixth year of being the rector of a parish in Washington, D.C. I was single. I was struggling with many faith questions while trying to serve as the rector of a struggling congregation that was unintentionally hosting one of Washington's largest drug markets. The congregation had its own internal conflicts. In February of 1993 I was diagnosed with breast cancer. I was devastated, mostly because I felt so alone. But I took cancer on as a project. I read. I researched. I had second and third opinions. I made treatment decisions. I had a close friend who went to every radiation treatment with me and every chemotherapy treatment with me and who took care of me in her home after those treatments. She was a life-saver. I worked through treatment. I developed close bonds with parishioners who were also dealing with cancer. I remember telling one family to call me anytime day or night. Their mother was dying of pancreatic cancer. One night around 2 a.m. they called and I went. We all sat around her bed and sang spirituals until she died. Several years later I saw one of her daughters who had been there that night. She said, "We often talk about you and Mom. We had never heard a white woman sing spirituals like you did!" It was indeed a privilege to be there, and I've never forgotten that night.

Chemotherapy, as many of you know, is cumulative. I was very sick during the last round of it. It was the first time I thought I might die, that it was a clear possibility. That night I heard a voice as clearly as I've heard any other. "Carlyle, you have nothing to fear in life or in death." I woke up the next morning and realized that in fact I was more afraid of really living than I was of dying. While being an early-ordained woman in the Episcopal church was risky, I was not risking, realizing, or being my true self. I was not able to say what I really wanted or able to act on it. I know now that I didn't have a clear, inner sense of self.

But that morning when I woke up, I got a yellow legal pad and wrote down in rank order what I wanted to do with my life. I wouldn't have been able to say it then, but I can say it now. I was coming to life, the spirit she was blowing!

Number one on my list was having an intimate relationship. I had not allowed myself to want that. Yes, I had relationships with men and with women, but I was not able to claim my need for intimacy. In fact, I was probably unaware of it. But somehow, by the presence of the spirit, I was no longer in the dark. I was ready to acknowledge want and ready to do something about it. Take real risks.

For two years I dated lots of different people, and I did something I'd never done before. I began to answer ads in the *Washington Post* and almost every other newspaper and magazine I could get my hands on. The first ads I answered were for men, and I went out with lots of different men. Then in 1995, my friend who had cared for me during treatment showed me an ad in *The Blade*, the gay and lesbian newspaper in D.C. It was a great ad, and we still have a copy of it. "My friends have told me to get a life. Therefore looking for..." I called the woman who had placed it and she told me so many people had answered the ad that she was having a party at the Cowboy Café in Arlington. Okay, I thought. I'm going. Until I got to the café. I hesitated, but I was committed, and I said to myself, I'm doing this. It was a big party, and about half an hour into it I looked across the table and saw this very interesting person. We began talking. I liked her, so I decided—following the risk-taking plan—to ask her out. This coming February we will celebrate twenty-five years together. She is with me in every conceivable way, and in particular, as it relates to this evening, as we deal with the two blood cancers that lurk within me. We go to Memorial Sloan Kettering every three months, and I would not be telling the truth if I said it has been easy for either one of us. But it is very doable, Sloan Kettering is great, and we try to have fun while we're in New York.

Recently, I listened to a Krista Tippett podcast. She was having a conversation with Esther Perel, a psychologist who has written a book on what she calls "erotic intelligence." This concept came to her as she and her husband listened to trauma survivors and as she thought about her own parents who were holocaust survivors. She wanted to know, "What does it mean to come back to life? What does it mean to face adversity and still take risks and live with joy?" She talked about eroticism as being alive not only in the context of sexuality but in the whole of life. She talked about desire as the ability to own our wanting and how it takes feeling worthy to acknowledge our needs and desires.

I've often wondered about the connection between sexuality and spirituality, or, more accurately, using her language, between eroticism and spirituality. Each is about coming to life, being alive, willing to take risks, willing to own our wanting. I believe that is the gift cancer gave me—the grace to own my own desire, my own wanting. And that gift gave me courage.

Finally, I want to say that there are two realities of my faith that inform me and have helped me enormously as I deal with cancer and a host of other things. The first is incarnation. Central to our faith is the belief that God became a person. Someone with skin. Again Barbara Brown Taylor is helpful here. She says:

> *After years of watching bodies being dug out of craters in Manhattan and caves in Afghanistan, after the body counts coming from Southeast Asia, Gaza, and Iraq, most of us could use a reminder that God does not come to us beyond the flesh but in the flesh, at the hands of a teacher who will not be spiritualized but who goes on trusting the embodied sacraments of bread, wine, water, and feet. "Do this," he said. Not believe this, but do this, "in remembrance of me."* (An Altar in the World, p. 44)

And second, as each of us knows very well, cancer or no cancer, being a human being is hard. No doubt about it. Because we are each vulnerable, weak, and have little or no control over outcomes. Each of us will die. But that is why I find Jesus so compelling. Long ago I read an article by Michael J. Buckley, titled "Because Beset with Weakness," a phrase that comes from Paul's letter to the Hebrews. He writes that weakness helps us relate to God because it is in moments of weakness that God is most likely to appear. The challenge to remain faithful comes to us when we feel like all we can do is just put one foot in front of the other.

In his book *Consolations*, David Whyte says that vulnerability is where we learn to become larger. We can mourn our losses or see them as opportunities for compassion. I believe we can do that no matter what happens, and that we can die well, when w are on a spiritual path that we practice day by day.

I believe we can do that no matter what happens, and that we can die well, when we are on a spiritual path we practice day by day.

Right Under Our Noses

*What is the kingdom of God like? And to what
should I compare it? It is like a mustard seed
that someone took and sowed in the garden;
it grew and became a tree, and the birds of
the air made nests in its branches.*

Luke 13:18-19

SOMETIMES I THINK JESUS JUST LIKED TO UPSET PEOPLE, OR AT least get a rise out of them. Or at the very least, he wanted them to see things a little differently—perhaps radically differently. Usually, the upsetting things he said were to religious people, those entrenched in their own views. Or, as in the case this morning, to his very own disciples.

Today, Jesus compares faith—faith that they and we might have—to a mustard seed. Just a short time ago he compared the kingdom of God to a mustard seed. Sounds innocuous enough to us, right? So what? A mustard seed. Hey, I've seen plenty of necklaces with mustard seeds in them. What's wrong with that? Why would that be upsetting?

Well, behind Jesus' use of the mustard seed as metaphor was

the reality that anyone in his time would have known. A mustard plant was a weed, something no one, absolutely no one, wanted in their garden. In fact, some of the religious people viewed mustard plants as unclean. At the very least, people would have seen mustard plants and their seeds as just terribly ordinary.

Jesus' comparison of the kingdom of heaven to a mustard seed made it sound terribly ordinary. Not the kingdom people expected, one of military might that would rid Israel of the Romans and return it to its former glory. A mustard seed, small, often unwanted. Certainly not powerful. Like our lives—yours and mine.

Jesus' disciples have been having difficulty with forgiveness. Who doesn't? They say to him in this morning's gospel, "Increase our faith!" In other words, show us, teach us, give us enough faith so that we can forgive. Seven times a day? I'm with the disciples here. Forgiveness is very difficult. But Jesus says if your faith is as small and as ordinary as a mustard seed, you can do almost anything, including forgiving someone who is difficult to forgive. Jesus says, "You don't need a flashy faith, just a little, ordinary faith, like a mustard seed."

Theologian Frederick Buechner says, "Faith is better understood as a verb than as a noun. As a process rather than a possession. It is on-again-off-again rather than once-and-for-all. Faith is not being sure where you're going, but going anyway. A journey without maps." That definition perfectly describes me forty years ago when I entered seminary. What was a woman going to do with a seminary education?

Actually, I like to think about faith as a gift because in my life faith is nothing that I have ever created or made happen. Faith has simply been a gift in my life. Often it is the power to continue being faithful even when faith means just putting one foot in front of the other. Faith to me is like love. I don't make it happen. It is a gift to be received and treasured.

Faith to me is like a sixth sense—not as in paranormal but as in ultra-normal. It is the gift of sight that sees the ordinary, that sees the hand of God in all things. It is the wonder of creation, including ourselves and others. It is the gift of seeing the sacred right under our noses. With such a gift, we can sometimes even do the hardest things—like forgiving each other!

Essence of a Person—Funeral of David Boyce

EACH OF US IS A NOTEBOOK, A FOLDER OF DATA—WHERE WE WERE BORN, where we went to school, when we married, what jobs we had. Much of that data is interesting and important, and much of it is forgettable.

Today we remember and celebrate the life of David Boyce. Yes, there's lots of data about Dave, but that's not what we miss, what we remember and treasure about this man. We miss his presence.

Dave Boyce made a lasting impression on everyone he met. It was Dave's presence—*who* he was and *how* he was—that touched us and is what we remember, celebrate, and hold dear today. Data is easy to describe. Presence is harder to describe but easier to see, to spot, and to feel. Dave had qualities of presence that were palpable, hard to miss, and very lovable.

Dave had a merry presence. There was a twinkle about him, almost as if he were the only person in on the joke. And, yes, he loved jokes and told them regularly, in a kind of offhand way. They weren't necessarily great jokes—some even fell flat. But you couldn't help but notice and feel how much he enjoyed telling them. I don't know how he came by this quality, this merry presence, but I saw it in him almost all the time, even when he was very ill. You can't fake merriment. It was deeply embedded in Dave's soul.

He had an uncanny ability, or rather grace, to attract children and dogs, and that too is a very telling presence. Children and dogs don't lie. You can't fool them. They know whether they are loved or not. You will see, if you haven't already, a wonderful picture of Dave with one of his grandchildren. This picture was posted on Facebook soon after he died. When I saw it, I thought, "There is the real Dave Boyce!" It captures the presence of real love in him. If a picture is better than a thousand words, this picture is better than a million. Elinor also shared with me a video of Dave posing, even dancing, as a Gummy Bear for his grandchildren. Dave knew how to play, as well as how to love.

Elinor and Dave often took care of our dog, Jackson, when we were away. Jackson loved being at their house. He would walk in the front door, head right to the kitchen where his water bowl was, have a drink, and jump into Dave's lap. Jackson was absolutely at home in Dave's lap, in that comforting, welcoming, and loving lap. One of my favorite pictures is that of Dave holding Jackson.

Dave had a quality and presence I can only call resilience— loving resilience. He lived with multiple myeloma for longer than many, and it did not stop him from volunteering with almost every organization in town from the Community Resource Center to the Tunnell Cancer Center to the Rehoboth Beach Film Society to the Rehoboth Art League.

Dave loved life. He and Elinor spent the greater part of last year traveling. On the back of your bulletin is a picture of Dave on one of their trips. He loved Elinor deeply and summoned the strength to share with her every moment of living he possibly could. He also made it a point to be in touch with others who were suffering. He did not let cancer keep him from being engaged.

A long time ago a wise soul said, "The two most important words in the English language are hello and good-bye." Saying hello to Dave Boyce, celebrating his life, his presence in this service, is wonderful. Saying goodbye is very hard.

Toward the end of this service Jeffrey Ross will say a prayer that commends Dave into the arms of a loving savior. While none of us has ever seen the physical embodiment of Jesus, many of us feel his loving presence. The presence of Dave Boyce— his merriment, his loving comfort, his strength and resilience and much more—is at rest in Jesus' loving arms. I believe that they are a match—a match made in heaven.

Welcomed

To be welcomed is to experience acceptance no matter who we are, where we have been, or where we are going. It does not depend on our circumstances, our actions, or our attitudes. The truth is that God loves us whoever and wherever we are, and the door to his kingdom is always open.

Turn Around, Look and See

From that time, Jesus began to proclaim,
"Repent, for the kingdom of heaven has come
near." As he walked by the Sea of Galilee, he saw
two brothers, Simon, who is called Peter, and
Andrew his brother, casting a net into the sea,
for they were fishermen. And he said to them,
"Follow me, and I will make you fish for people."
Matthew 4: 17-19

SOME PREACHERS GIVE THE SAME SERMON AGAIN AND AGAIN.
Really? we might ask. Have they run out of material? Hit a spiritual dry spot? Or perhaps this one sermon says it all. Jesus actually had one sermon. We heard it in Matthew's gospel this morning. It is repeated in Luke and Mark as well as again in Matthew. I think it's found in the gospels at least twenty times. That's a lot of the same sermon for such a short preaching career.

And, it's a short sermon. No longer than a tweet on Twitter. Here it is: *Repent, for the kingdom of God has come near.* That's it. That's the sermon. According to Matthew, these are the first words on Jesus' lips after his baptism and forty days in the wilderness with the devil.

But before we look at the content of this sermon, it's important to explore the meaning of preaching, because on the lips of some preachers, this sermon could mean something entirely different.

Preaching actually has gotten a bad name. It has come to mean for many of us a kind of moralism, a high-handed way of telling us what to do and how to be. Preaching in this context is akin to harping, hammering home the same point. But actually, the verb "to preach" comes from the Greek *logizomai*, which means "to word." We "word" people all the time. Think of raising children. When we "word" a child smart or beautiful, princess or prince, this child becomes smart or beautiful, princess or prince. It works the opposite way too, as some of us know only too painfully. I know a woman who is very thin but whose mother told her constantly as a child that she was fat. Even though she is still thin and very attractive and now fifty-seven, she still believes that she is fat. Words, how we "word" each other, are very powerful.

Jesus is laying a word on us this morning. Preaching. Not harping, not moralizing, not telling us how we ought to be. But laying a word on us. Jesus is not saying, "Listen, you gotta clean up your act, improve, become a better person because God doesn't like you the way you are, and God is up there watching your every move." Jesus is saying, true to the Aramaic which he spoke, "Repent. Turn around. Look. See. The presence of God is near. Close at hand." The presence of God is here and now. Not up there. Not far away. Not dependent on how good you are. But simply here. Now.

That's really enough of a sermon, isn't it? What many of us long to hear, need to hear. Aren't many of us searching for just this, the presence, the reality of God? Jesus is saying the holy is in our midst. We don't need to work on ourselves to receive it. We don't need to do a lot of good works to deserve it. All we need to do is look around. Look. See. The response to that sermon might simply be, "Wow."

What Jesus shows us in parable after parable, story after story, is that no one is outside God's presence, God's realm, the kingdom. From this reality, the reality of God's presence close at hand, all else follows—love of God, love of self, love of neighbor, love of enemy.

The call of the disciples, embedded in today's gospel, is nothing less than Jesus' invitation to come and see. It is as if Jesus says to Peter, Andrew, James, and John, "Come. Come with me. Let me show you the presence of God in your midst. Turn around. Look and see. You will see it everywhere, especially where you least expect. In those who are sick, in those who screw up, in those left by the side of the road, in those viewed as untouchable, in those who help them. Even in my own suffering and death." This is our call too, those of us gathered in Jesus' name, Jesus' presence, the church.

How? How we might ask? How can we learn to turn around, to see? I imagine Jesus might answer with what is at the heart of his other, longer sermon, the sermon on the mount—prayer. Not the "please God, take X away," or "please God, give me Y," but prayer as Simone Weil defined it—paying attention. Seeing. Or prayer as many over the millennia have known, a loving relationship with God whose center is everywhere and whose circumference is nowhere. "Abiding," as the author of John's gospel puts it, or as Franciscan Richard Rohr says, "Prayer is like practicing heaven now."

The Washington National Cathedral recently sponsored a week of experiential prayer called "Seeing Deeper: Come and See." They removed all the chairs from the cavernous cathedral nave. Some people were doing yoga, some were sitting in Centering Prayer, some were doing tai-chi, some were walking the labyrinth, some were singing. A friend went and said it was a wonderful experience. She is a prayer-full person and a lover of choral music, and the experience of many different forms of prayer in one place reminded her of a choral conductor who said, "Imagine that there is a chorus being sung all the time, just beyond our hearing, and when you sing, you are joining that invisible chorus."

Kind of like today's one sentence sermon: "Repent. Turn around. The presence of God is near." Close. Here and now. See deeper. Join the chorus of angels and archangels and all the company of heaven. Holy. Holy. Holy. Heaven and earth are full of your glory.

Give us grace to answer the call, to turn around, see, know that the presence of God is near, close, here, now.

I Need a Good Shepherd

"I am the good shepherd. The good
shepherd lays down his life for the sheep."
John 10:11

THERE ARE SOME VERY SIMPLE ASPECTS TO THE GOSPEL STORY we just heard. The questioners have questions that could be *our* questions, either ones we have now or have had in years past. "How long will you keep us in suspense? If you are the Messiah, tell us plainly!" How many of us might have asked, or rather demanded, that of Jesus? Our questions might go something like, "Okay, Jesus, pony up. Is it true or not? Are you God in the flesh? A simple yes or no will do. Or are you something that people made up hundreds of years ago? We need to know. Speak plainly!" Haven't you had that question? I know a clergy colleague who says, "I've spent my entire life working for someone I've never seen!"

But Jesus' answer to his questioners is not so simple, or at least I don't think so. And his answer sounds rather un-Jesus-like—rough, curt, quick. Jesus says to his questioners, "The works that I do in my father's name testify to me; but you do not believe because you do not belong to my sheep." Whoa! I suppose if I had been there, I might be just a little perplexed if not downright hurt. "Because you do not belong to my sheep?????" I'd want to know, so how come I don't belong? Is this just some capricious act on God's part? Some are included and some aren't for no apparent reason? How does this happen? Is it just because some believe and others don't? How did they get to believe in the first place? Speak plainly, Jesus! "Is belief a gift or is it work? Rather than go into a systematic theological history of Augustinian theology vs. Pelagian, I'm going to tell you a story. My story.

My sister, Carolyn, is not a church-goer. She will only come to church on Christmas day and that's because I am preaching. Otherwise, she would never go to church because she does not, cannot, believe that Jesus is God in the flesh. None of my once-a-year sermons on the wonder of Incarnation has convinced her otherwise. Oh well, so much for the folly of what we preach. My sister says she can't come to church because she can't say the creed. Okay, I say, just hum during the parts you don't believe, or hum during the whole thing for that matter. But that's never been a very satisfactory suggestion for Carolyn.

But still I wonder, especially in light of today's gospel story, why is it that two people raised in the same household, with the same parents, with the same family dysfunction and family glory, why is it that one of us is not a believer and one of us is? And one of us has given the greater part of her life to the enterprise? Did God somehow say, "Well, that Carlyle Gill needs all the help she can get, so let's give her belief and a place in the sheepfold. And her sister Carolyn seems to be doing just fine on her own so we won't bother her with believing"?

I really have given this some thought over the past week. And here's what I think. I absolutely don't think God is that capricious. I think the difference between me and my sister (and there are many, theological and otherwise) is that early on in my life I knew at some level, some profound level, that I *needed* a good shepherd, that I *needed* to belong to someone who cared for me no matter what. That I could truly belong somewhere since I feared that I didn't, couldn't belong anywhere. That someone knew me by name, using the Hebrew understanding of name which means presence. That someone knew my presence, my essence, knew me through and through like the author of Psalm 139. It's that simple, I think. I needed and still need, now more consciously, a good shepherd. Someone who will lead me beside the still waters. Someone who will restore my soul. And most importantly, someone who will walk through the valley of the shadow of death with me.

Yes, I've studied a lot of theology, and I love it. Theology— learning about, loving God—is my heart's desire. But I am not a believer because I've studied it and intellectually assent to it. I am a believer because I *need* a good shepherd. And I want to hang out with all the other sheep who need one too. I am eternally grateful to this good shepherd and eternally grateful that I am in the sheepfold with all of you.

Yes, the King of Love, my Shepherd is.

Just Say "Yes"

He said also to the one who had invited him,
"When you give a luncheon or a dinner, do not
invite your friends or your brothers or your
relatives or rich neighbors, in case they may
invite you in return, and you would be repaid.
But when you give a banquet, invite the poor
and the crippled, the lame and the blind.
Luke 14: 12-13

OH, THE TEXTS THIS MORNING! THEY ARE CHALLENGING. JERE-
miah doesn't mince words, never does. He says in so many words,
"Thus says the lord, you have screwed up!" Jesus is from that same
prophetic tradition, but he uses parables to make a point just as
strongly. Jesus' parables have a way of sneaking up on you. On the
surface, the gospel this morning may sound like advice on how
to give a successful dinner party. But no. This is not advice. This
is a searing critique.

Jesus' parables about the banquet both as guest and host strike
squarely at the honor/shame culture of first century Judaism as
well as the firmly held purity code, the code that names who is
in and who is out.

In this morning's gospel, Jesus continues to shock. Jesus again treads difficult and dangerous territory. He essentially calls out the guests for assuming places of honor when in fact they should assume places of humility. Then Jesus admonishes the host of this banquet by saying that the invited guests should be the least, the outsiders, the blind, the poor, the crippled. All of this in the context of a sabbath meal hosted by a leader of the Pharisees.

The impact of Jesus' parables is shock and provocation because of what was (and is) life in the presence of God, in God's realm, God's kingdom. What was at stake was inclusion. Who is wrapped into God's loving arms? Only the well and the wealthy? The privileged?

All of this is set in the context of a sabbath meal and sabbath worship, the place that represents and celebrates God's presence, God's realm, God's kingdom. It is here that Jesus calls out exclusivity and privilege. I used to think I got the exclusivity/privilege part. I came to the table, to the presence, to the church, from a place of vulnerability and exclusion as a woman and as a closeted lesbian. I heard the gospel from that place. I knew myself to be an outsider and knew that I was welcomed, invited, loved, even if the church of the nineteen-seventies had not yet caught up with the good news of inclusion.

This reality of inclusion is true for many of us. We are not here on Sunday morning because we have nothing better to do. We are here because we are vulnerable, having a hard time being human beings. Some of us have lost people most dear to us.

Some of us have received a diagnosis that has us in shock. All of us need companions, community, a place to be. We are the poor, the crippled, the lame, and the blind in the wilderness "a leanin' on the lord," as my friend Verna Dozier used to say.

But even knowing that, knowing that about myself, knowing my own vulnerability and my outsider state, I too am awakened and shocked by Jesus' parables. I am drawn to this text and shaken by this text because this parable makes me aware of my privilege as a white person. I experience inclusion in many places based solely on the color of my skin. I am, to use Jesus' banquet story, a guest who can assume a place of honor just because of that, and I am often not even aware of it. All the while I am thinking I am a very humble person and one of the least. That is mind bending!

So, Jesus' parables have worked. I am provoked. Shaken. Seeing something new and disturbing. But there is more, much more. Being shaken and provoked is not enough.

The root meaning of the word parable is from the Greek, *parabolein*, which means thrown alongside. There is a reality that Jesus wants us to know, to see what is thrown alongside, near us, next to us. Jesus' imagery of a wedding banquet is purposeful. He wants us to see, to know, that at the heart of reality there is a banquet, the marriage of heaven and earth, an essential unity to which we are all invited, joyfully invited—to know and to live from. Here at this wedding banquet is true inclusion and true humility because at this table we are in the presence. It doesn't matter who we are, whether we have just lost the love of our life, received an awful diagnosis, or are struggling with any of the many difficulties of being human. The color of our skin at this marriage of heaven and earth, at this essential unity, doesn't matter. For we are one, and it is from this place that everything is and can be different.

The physicists know this. The tiniest particles in the universe demonstrate that we live in a UNI-verse. The mystics among us know this. Jesus knows this and wants us to know it too. Seeing participating in the wedding banquet that is right before our eyes is IT. Saying yes to the invitation is all that matters. Saying yes can make all the difference. Saying no is the real human tragedy. The gospel story that follows this one says just that—we are all invited to the wedding banquet.

Just say, "YES!"

And there, you have it. Truly. There we have it, at this banquet.

We Are All Saints

*When Jesus saw the crowds, he went up
the mountain; and after he sat down, his
disciples came to him. Then he began to
speak, and taught them, saying....*
Matthew 5:1-2

MY FAMILY, PERHAPS LIKE YOURS, HAD A FAMILY ALBUM—AN old black-covered thing barely held together by shoelaces, with pictures in little black corners that kept them in the album. The pictures were old —way old—and yellowed, but they were wonderful to me because they were my relatives. I had heard stories about them from my parents, and I just loved looking at them.

There was my father's father—Tilgin. I think his name was a word they made up to describe his irascible nature. He was a character—he had tilgin. And he sired another character, my father, who sired what some say was another character—me.

This Sunday we are looking in the family album called the church, the living record of those who have gone before us and those who are with us still. The temptation we have when looking at this album is to think these relatives were really good people who did really great things. And, therefore, we think we aren't so good and can't do such great things.

Okay, there's St. Francis who gave away his rich heritage and lived as a mendicant preaching to the birds (well, maybe not so different from some of my relatives). But then there's Bishop Tutu who, instead of wanting to punish those who had tortured and discriminated against black South Africans, wanted to hear the truth from them and to forgive them! Now, there's an outrageous act. Saintly, some would say. Or Dorothy Day who founded The Catholic Worker, seeking justice for the poor. She said, "Don't call me a saint. I don't want to be dismissed that easily." Or the woman most of us have never heard of who spent her life doing others' laundry. Osceola McCarty from Hattiesburg, Mississippi, a black woman with no education, did this for seventy-five years. When she was 85 she gave her life savings, $150,000, to the University of Southern Mississippi for black scholarships. When asked why she didn't spend it on herself, she said "I *am* spending it on myself." Or there is the pastor of a Lutheran church in Salisbury who has taken a small, dying Lutheran church and made it the epicenter of welcome for all people. Three weeks ago, Faith Lutheran Church hosted Salisbury's first interfaith coming-out day called *Here I Am, God*. The Lutheran pastor told her own coming out story in the form of a poem.

Now much of the time it's easy for us to look at the church's family album and say, "Aren't they great? Aren't they good people?

I could never be like that." Or, as my mother used to say, "Isn't she a saint?" By that she meant the person was good, had great table manners, always wrote prompt thank-you notes, and did good works on the side. I always knew I was not in that category. I suspected that I had some of that tilgin energy from my grandfather and that wasn't so saintly.

But if another saint, Saint Paul, is to be believed, goodness has nothing to do with saintliness. That's right. That's what Paul said. Goodness has nothing to do with saintliness. He even wrote to those pesky congregants who were in so much trouble in Corinth fighting over this and that, addressing them as the Saints in Corinth. For Paul, sainthood and holiness were givens—God given. Sainthood is the work of God given to all of us, he said. And he ought to have known since he was so clear about his own dark side. He claimed to be a Pharisee, and was among the best, until he was shocked and stunned into knowing in his bones that he was loved just as he was.

And that's what you and I need to know and absorb deep into our bones—that we are loved just as we are. We are saints because God chooses to see us that way. God chooses to name us beloved, precious, God's very own. In Baptism we are marked as Christ's own forever. First thing. Not after we've earned it or gotten some advanced degree in being religious.

The bottom line to this day is that we are—each and every one of us—saints. This is ALL Saints Day, and all the saints are right here. You. Me. Plus, all the saints who have gone before us (my mother, even Grandfather Tilgin, your people, and the ones named in the prayers today who have died this year). A great, great cloud of witnesses. This is what we invoke at the altar when we say, "With angels and archangels and all the company of heaven."

This is the power of God, the resurrection power of God. The same power that shouted to Lazarus to come out of the tomb, to come alive. And this is the power conferred on all saints known as the church, to unbind all the Lazaruses of this world and let them go. We are given the charge to unbind, to forgive, and to embody the grace we have received. And this power does create and will continue to create a new heaven and a new earth.

Here's a great quote from my favorite Episcopal preacher, Barbara Brown Taylor, who says in one paragraph what has taken me eight.

> *Once you are baptized, you belong to God and all that remains to be seen is*
> *what you will do about it. Just remember that you do not have to be famous,*
> *or perfect, or dead. You just have to be you—the one-of-a-kind, never-to-be-repeated human being whom God created you to be—to love as you are loved, to throw*
> *your arms around the world, to shine like the sun. (Home by Another Way, p. 212)*

This is why we come to church, whether we've been here a hundred years or just got here ten minutes ago. We are not here to learn how to be good. We are here to learn that we are loved, that we are God's saints, beloved and precious in his sight. I can tell you that knowing this has forever changed my life.

Peter's People

Then he began to teach them that the Son
of Man must undergo great suffering, and
be rejected by the elders, the chief priests,
and the scribes, and be killed, and after
three days rise again. He said all this quite
openly. And Peter took him aside and
began to rebuke him.

Then Peter began to speak to them. "I truly
understand that God shows no partiality...."
Mark 8:31-32 and Acts 10:34

WE ARE CELEBRATING WHAT IS CALLED OUR "PATRONAL FESTIVAL."
Actually, we share it with the Washington National Cathedral,
which is named the Cathedral of Saints Peter and Paul. June 29
is the actual feast day for those two saints, but the preacher (that
would be me) chose to move it to this Sunday.

As the church of St. Peter's, we are actually Peter's people.
What does that mean? What does that look like? What impli-
cations does that name have for us now? This sermon will be a
short look at those questions. While the biblical story does not
focus on personality the way our culture does, I will still try to

paint a short picture of this man so we can have some sense of what it means to be Peter's people.

Peter, actually Simon Bar Jonah, was an energetic and successful fisherman, a hard worker in the family fishing business. But when Jesus called him to follow, he quickly dropped those fishing nets and followed. A quick decision maker, to say the least, and a bit of a risk taker. Who knew where following this Jesus might lead? But Peter was game and I imagine he thought that following Jesus would lead to some kind of grand success. I imagine Peter really wanted to make a difference in the world—like many of us—and following Jesus looked like a way to do that. So, in today's gospel story things are looking good for Peter. He actually gets his heart's desire—the right answer! When Jesus asks, "Who do you say that I am?" Peter aces the quiz. "You are the messiah!" (Matthew 16:13-16).

But we know just a few paragraphs later in Matthew's gospel, after Jesus warns the disciples that he will suffer and die, that Peter objects. "No, no. No. Not that. No suffering for you, Jesus, or for me. We are going to be successful here. Strong. Winners. Most likely to succeed."

Peter, like many of us, does not, cannot, believe that suffering of any kind can be part of the plan. It's almost as though we believe that at birth we got some sort of contract with God that said, "Listen, I will do all the right things, and you will keep me safe." But when something untoward happens—like illness or death or failure—we say, "Where were you God? Why didn't you save me? Why didn't you save the person I love? Why did you let this happen?"

I think some version of this contract was in Peter's mind. So, when the predicted suffering came, Peter couldn't handle it. "I do not know the man!" he shouted (Matthew 26:72). Three times.

All that Peter had hoped for, had built his dreams upon, was crushed on the cross. Jesus was dead. He had been killed at the hands of the state and his own faith tradition. It was one of those crushing moments many of us have experienced. We have lost and we suffer.

However, I believe suffering is the very crucible of faith. It was not Peter's right answers that gave him faith. It was not his position as number one disciple that gave him faith. It was his suffering.

I believe that lasting impact can be seen in one core sentence on the lips of Peter recorded in Paul's letter to the church in Corinth. That one sentence is "I believe that God shows no partiality." Or, as it has been translated through the years, "God's embrace is wide." Or as a former presiding bishop of the Episcopal Church said, "There are no outcasts."

This one sentence on the lips of Peter, "I believe that God shows no partiality," saved the early church as it haggled over who was in and who was out, and it continues to save the church to this day. Coming to this wisdom was not easy or simple for Peter. Nor is it for you or for me. This is the wisdom born of loss, suffering, and grace. It is the wisdom that comes from losing ourselves to find ourselves. It is nothing less than the way of the cross.

This wisdom is at the heart of this community named St. Peter's. We are Peter's people. We are an inclusive community where there are no outcasts, a community that embodies Peter's wisdom. We put those words of Peter into action. Thousands and thousands of dollars flow annually from this church to help the lives of people struggling in this community through the Community Resource Center and beyond. Children of all backgrounds are fed and, more importantly, known by countless members of this church. The overwhelming experience of people coming into this church is that of welcome. It certainly was my experience almost ten years ago.

We are living through a time when being Peter's people matters greatly. The world appears to be drawing in, closing out those considered "other" and living in fear. But as Peter's people, we live inside that one sentence: "I believe that God shows no partiality." We are learning its wisdom, practicing its presence, and giving those words flesh. To be Peter's people, to embody God's wide embrace, is saving. And not only for ourselves but also for all those whom we touch.

Come, You Are Welcome

He said also to the one who had
invited him, "When you give a
luncheon or dinner, do not invite
your friends or your brothers or
your relatives or rich neighbors,
in case they may invite you in
return, and you would be repaid.
But when you give a banquet,
invite the poor, the crippled, the
lame, and the blind."
Luke 14:12-13

WHEN I WAS A KID, MY MOTHER USED TO SAY TO ME, "CARLYLE, you should be nice to everyone because you never know, you might be entertaining an angel unaware." She thought that quote was from Shakespeare, but no, it's from whoever wrote the letter to the Hebrews we just heard. But my mother was pretty close to the actual letter to the Hebrews that reads, "Do not neglect to show hospitality to strangers, for by doing that some have entertained angels without knowing it." Angels, according to the biblical story, are messengers, messengers sent by God, bearing the presence of God.

Well, I had lunch with an angel last week who told me an amazing story. She called it an epiphany. Her story was all about having the felt experience that she was and is included at the table, the banquet that Jesus is talking about in today's gospel story. For years she had been carrying around a sense of unworthiness, a sense of shame, that somehow as a divorced Roman Catholic she was not welcome at the table, at the banquet.

She is not alone. This is the story of many of us who have been hurt, shamed, excluded from the table, the banquet, the wedding feast as Jesus calls it in today's gospel. I know someone who was told she could not receive communion until she renounced her sexual orientation.

In his parable delivered to the Pharisees in today's gospel, Jesus is describing nothing less than the marriage of heaven and earth, grace beyond measure. The list of those excluded from the banquet is long, and the real shame belongs to Pharisaic Judaism as well as some of today's churches who continue to exclude people of color, gay and lesbian people, women, people with physical and emotional disabilities, people who are homeless. The list is long and sad and totally contrary to Jesus' teaching in today's gospel story and in countless others.

Jesus' radical welcome is at the core of Luke's gospel, at the core of the good news itself. It has not been easy for the church as institution to practice welcome because it is not easy for most of us to embrace all that is within us, all our fears of being different or other. Actually, hatred and its consequence—exclusion—is nothing less than fear and shame turned outward. We cannot embrace on the outside what we have excluded on the inside.

And I think that is why Jesus speaks so often about welcome. Why Jesus' stories revolve around inclusion, whether it's the tax collector, or the woman who crashes Simon the Pharisee's dinner, or the little boy with epilepsy, or the woman at the well, or even his own followers who manage to screw up on a regular basis. Peter, to be specific.

Jesus' good news is not about perfection, morality, or manners. It's about radical welcome. This message has transforming power because it takes very difficult, firmly rooted emotions and attitudes, all the "not good enough" stuff we carry inwardly and says, "No matter who you are, you are welcome at this table." And more, as we look ahead in Luke's gospel story about dinner parties, Jesus says, "I will send out a search party to find you and bring you to this amazing banquet where you will learn that you are loved just as you are."

The search party that comes to seek you and me, that wants us to come to the banquet to participate in God's abundance and grace is made up of angels. They are God's messengers that we are entertaining unaware. The woman I had lunch with last week met her angel by accident (really?) on a beach in a so-called chance encounter. This meeting allowed her to recognize and begin to let go of the guilt and shame she had been carrying.

The wonder of this liturgy is that this banquet, this sacrament of welcome called Eucharist is celebrated every Sunday. It is nothing less than the outward and visible sign of Jesus' welcome to all of us. Communion: the marriage of heaven and earth, the grace of inclusion in Christ's body. Our challenge is to accept this welcome into our bodies and take it into a world that needs it desperately.

I will close with these words from the Iona Community Prayerbook.

> *This is the altar not of the church but of the Lord. It is made ready for those who love him and those who want to love him more. So come, all you who have much faith and you who have very little, you who have been here often and those who have not been here long. Those who have tried to follow and those who have failed. Come, because it is the lord who welcomes you. It is his will that those who find him should find him here. Amen.*

Loopholes

A certain ruler asked him, "Good teacher,
what must I do to inherit eternal life?"
Luke 18:18

It is said that W.C. Fields was once poring over the gospels. Someone who found this behavior out of character asked him what he was doing. He reportedly replied, "I'm looking for loopholes."

When many of us hear this morning's gospel text, we are also rushing for loopholes. Surely Jesus didn't mean it. It must be a metaphor for something. I don't really have to give away everything I've worked so hard for in order to have eternal life. Do I?

I think Jesus actually meant it. He knew that the earnest rich man who came to him asking what he must do to inherit eternal life really did want that. He wanted to have eternal life along with all the other things he had. He wanted evidence that he was okay, successful, secure, independent, and assured a place in heaven.

We, truth be told, are not much different than the rich man. We want evidence—and more—we want to hang on to our evidence. We want to be successful, secure, independent, and assured of a place in heaven. We want the answers to our questions, especially our spiritual questions. We want to be sure we are right, that we have taken the correct path that will one day lead us to having eternal life.

Every month I meet with two friends, accomplished men now in their 80s who are on a very genuine spiritual path. They, as it is said, do not need binoculars to see the end, and they want the answers before they die. I think they assume I have them! We have been meeting for over a year. I taught them the discipline of Centering Prayer at our last meeting. Last week they told me they just couldn't do it. They couldn't sit and do nothing They couldn't deal with a spiritual discipline that was fundamentally about letting go. They needed more structure. More answers. And I understand that. Centering Prayer isn't for everyone. But the more I've thought about it, the more I believe this gospel story is for them—and for us.

I believe Jesus meant exactly what he said because he wanted to say in the starkest terms, terms that would shock the rich man and us, terms that would be the most upsetting, that eternal life was not in the evidence or answers or the stuff that makes us feel successful and secure. He wanted to say that eternal life was not to be found in what we have amassed either materially or spiritually. Eternal life—the last thing the rich man wanted to acquire—is a gift, a quality of being, an openness to the presence of God that cannot be bought or earned or even fully understood. Eternal life can only be *received* as a gift. But the rich man couldn't receive it because he was grasping, clinging too tightly to his stuff, his evidence, his material and spiritual riches. The core of his issue was in his question. "What must I do to inherit eternal life?" He had spent his life doing. He was good at it. What must he do now? His question reminds me of Frederick Buechner's definition of grace. "There is *nothing* you have to do. There is nothing you *have* to do. There is nothing you have to *do*."

Henri Nouwen, well-known writer about the spiritual life, wrote a book about prayer called *With Open Hands*. The book's cover is simply a pair of open hands. I believe that Jesus is telling the rich man and us that the key to eternal life is opening our hands, letting go, receiving a gift, a gift beyond measure, one we cannot earn.

The clue to this gift is the way Jesus looks at the rich man— with love. Jesus is giving him the gift of eternal life right then and there, the unconditional, grace-filled love of God. *This* is eternal life.

But the rich man cannot receive it. He is the only person in scripture who walks away, truly and deeply empty-handed, with all his stuff.

The great irony in this story is that for most of us, it is far easier to give away all we have than it is to be open and receptive to the gift of eternal life—the unconditional love of God. At least if we give away all our stuff, we're *doing* something! And looking good in the process.

Notice, also, that Jesus does not run after the man and beg him to receive the gift of eternal life. He does not coerce him in any way to accept this gift. It wouldn't be a gift then. Love does not insist on its own way, as St. Paul says so well in First Corinthians.

Jesus wants the same for each of us, wants to give us this gift, the grace of eternal life, the knowledge and experience of God's unconditional love for us, the knowledge that, as St. Paul put it, "nothing can separate us from the love of God."

All we have to do is open, let go of our tight grasp on our stuff. Open our hands and our hearts. Receive.

And even if we can't do that, like the rich man, we are loved anyway. We just don't have the joy of knowing it.

Who Is This God?

The Pharisee, standing by himself,
was praying thus: "God, I thank you
that I am not like the other people—
thieves, rogues, adulterers, or even
like this tax collector. I fast twice a
week; I give a tenth of my income."
But the tax collector, standing far off,
would not even look up to heaven, but
was beating his breast and saying,
"God, be merciful to me, a sinner."
Luke 18:11-13

JESUS JUST SEEMS INTENT ON IRRITATING US. THIS MORNING'S gospel story is no exception. When I read it to the Wednesday evening Eucharist folks here at St. Peter's last week, one person was clearly very upset. "I'm tired of the Pharisees getting such a bad rap," she said. "It just seems that Jesus only cares for the people who screw up, not the people who are trying to lead decent lives. I mean, look at the prodigal son. He screwed up and got a party! Or this tax collector today who goes home justified. I just don't get it. It's not fair."

At the time, I couldn't think of much to say in response to her complaint. So I decided to say something like, "It does seem that way." Because it does. Jesus does seem to side with the outcast, the marginal people, even those who screw up royally. But since then, I've given the issue further thought.

Yes, it's true. Pharisees worked hard at being good people. They tried as hard as they could to keep the laws—all three hundred plus of them. You gotta hand it to them! Any rector of an Episcopal church would love to have a few Pharisees who tithed… I think.

And yes, it's true that tax collectors were held in very low regard, with contempt, actually. And for good reason. They conspired with the enemy. They turned against their own people to collect taxes for the Romans, for the occupiers. They did this for personal gain, and they were regarded as scum by their own.

So, why, then, as the person Wednesday evening asked, why then does Jesus say the tax collector goes home justified? What about the Pharisee who's been working at being right with God his entire life? It doesn't seem fair.

This parable is set in the context of a teaching about prayer begun last week with the woman who pesters the unjust judge. Jesus is essentially saying that prayer in all its aspects is about our relationship with God, who we are in the presence of God and who God is in our presence. Last week we learned that we can be as persistent in the presence of God as the woman was before the judge. This week we learn something else about our relationship with God, about prayer.

The Pharisee comes before God to chat about how good he is, what good he has done, how thankful he is that he's not like those thieves, adulterers, and especially that despised tax collector. The tax collector comes before God knowing that there is nothing, absolutely nothing, that justifies him, that makes him right in the eyes of God. He is probably embarrassed and mortified to be there in the first place. There is nothing he can boast about in the presence of God.

So, this parable asks us, you and me, who we are in the presence of God. Who are we? Really? Are we self-satisfied, or do we come needing God's grace?

This is a dangerous and tricky parable for religious people, for seekers of any kind. A few weeks ago, I led a five-day Centering Prayer retreat. These retreats are wonderful because they give us the opportunity to go deeper in our relationship with God and to the felt experience of God's presence and action in our lives. But the danger is that we can come out of such retreats feeling that we have something others don't have. Like the evangelical bumper sticker said—I FOUND IT!

A week later I was at a Buddhist retreat. A man got up to ask the retreat leader a question, and it was clear he was not posing a question but telling the leader and us what a better Buddhist he was! Not all that different from the Pharisee. Pharisees can be found everywhere!

This Pharisaical behavior, no matter where it is found, is very understandable. Who wants to admit to God or anyone else how vulnerable we are? What really lurks underneath all our good works? And, who among us doesn't feel smug every once in a while, thanking God we are not like those other poor souls?

The good news embedded in all of Jesus' parables is that we are—each one of us—beloved as we are. Just like the hymn, "Just as I am without one plea." Beloved before we've done anything good. Before we've straightened up our act. Beloved before we've hidden that part of ourselves about which we are most ashamed. Beloved while we are lost, vulnerable, afraid, other. Beloved just as we are. No matter what. I agree with the woman Wednesday evening. This kind of love is outrageous. This God is outrageous.

That same Godly love is directed to the Pharisee. The difference is he doesn't know he needs it. And therefore, he is profoundly lonely, with no real relationship to God or anyone else. He has no awareness of the wideness of God's mercy. And therefore, he is most to be pitied, way more than thieves, adulterers, and tax collectors.

So, the question at the heart of today's parable remains—who are we in the presence of God? And more, who is this God? A harsh judge to be pleased at all costs? Or one who loves us just as we are?

Curve Balls

Then Jesus said, "There was a
man who had two sons."
Luke 15:11

THE LITERAL MEANING OF THE WORD PARABLE—FROM THE
Greek *parabolein*—is "thrown alongside." In other words, a parable
is a curve ball. No major league player could throw them quite like
Jesus. They weren't thrown randomly but with purpose, largely
to question the Pharisees' and our assumptions about ourselves,
and, most importantly, our assumptions about God.

These parables, these curve balls, seem to come out of nowhere
and whiz right by us. They often seem puzzling. To those who
first heard them, especially those of the religious establishment,
they were scandalous, wild pitches to be stopped at all costs. This
curve ball pitcher had to be gotten rid of, traded at a minimum,
because these parables could undermine the faith.

Today's parable is well-known. This story of the prodigal son is
perhaps the best known of the gospel parables, and that is dangerous in itself because we *think* we know it, we *think* we know what

it means. We assume we know what Jesus is talking about—who the good guys are and who the bad guys are. But perhaps this parable still has a little curve in it, some surprise. Maybe it can still undermine our faith.

In the story, a son demands his inheritance. Never, ever, done before the death of a parent. Not then, not now. But the father, unlike the other patriarchs of the day, gives it to him. The son then takes the land he has been given and sells it, departing for a foreign country. Even in the initial transaction the father is disgraced in the eyes of his community because one of his sons abandons the family with some of its assets in hand and then spends it on loose living! More disgrace.

This son doesn't invest it, earning more money to bring home to his father, making everyone proud of his entrepreneurial skills. Instead, this son is left feeding pigs and reduced to eating what the pigs eat. No good Jew would ever, ever, do that.

Meanwhile, the other son is at home, dutifully doing what children did in those days—helping his father with chores. doing what was expected of him. *He* would never have asked for his inheritance while his father was alive. And now that inheritance is diminished because his shameless brother has lost much of it. This dutiful brother would never, I mean never, engage in loose living of any kind!

But then the first son returns—disheveled, dirty, skinny, poor, shamed, with nothing. And to everyone's amazement, the father runs out to the brow of the hill, even before his son is within shouting distance. When the son finally appears, the father throws his arms around him and welcomes him back home. "Welcome, welcome, welcome," he cries. "How good to have you back! Here, take this robe of mine, my very finest. Here, take this ring of mine, the symbol of my rule in this household. Let's party! Get the fatted calf! We will invite the entire family and the whole neighborhood to celebrate your return. I am so, so glad you are home again. You were lost, but now you are found."

The dutiful son is totally appalled. Who wouldn't be? Perhaps appalled is too weak a descriptor for how he feels. How, how could his father do this? How could his father welcome this no-good son back? "He has squandered his inheritance and his life. He has not been here to help his father and me. He has not followed the rules. He has shamed the family. Yet my father is giving him everything! His robe, his ring, and the fatted calf! This is outrageous. I will have none of it. Someone has to stand up for family values."

This curve ball of a parable was told to religious people, to the Pharisees who had kept the rules, who went to temple regularly, who lived by the purity code, who did the right things, who would never, ever, engage in loose living or associate with those who did, who did not collude with the occupying Romans by collecting taxes, who were outraged that Jesus ate with these sinners and tax collectors.

This curve ball of a parable was thrown alongside the Pharisees' deeply held assumptions about the nature of God and the nature of spirituality. God, to them, was a force to be reckoned with, a force to be pleased, a force that demanded goodness, a force who doled out reward and punishment.

And, lest we think this assumption about the nature of God no longer lives among us, let's think again. The curve ball is whizzing by! Many of us have a secret contract with God that goes something like this—if I do X, God will do Y. This usually means, "If I am good, keep the rules, then God will keep me safe and won't let anything bad happen to me or to anyone I love." We don't know we've made this contract until something bad does happen to us. Countless people have said to me, "I've done all the right things. I've said my prayers daily. How could God do this to me?"

Webster's defines prodigal as "wastefully or recklessly extravagant." And so, the heart of today's curve ball thrown by Jesus is that the real prodigal is God. God is not the great rewarder in the sky but an absolutely loving presence who welcomes us—all of us—no matter what. There is no contract to be with this God, no "if I do X, you will do Y." For this God, the only words are "welcome, welcome, welcome."

This curve ball of a parable has just as much power to convert today as it did then. I was reading in the *Washington Post* about a group of Christians determined to make the Supreme Court uphold DOMA, the Defense of Marriage Act. They said, "We need to decide whether we are a Christian nation or a pagan nation and get on with it. The glory of a nation lies in its righteousness." Well, that set me right off. There they go again, I thought. Giving Christianity a bad name, totally misunderstanding the meaning of righteousness. It means right relationship with God, and they're not in it.

Oops! Aren't I just like the dutiful brother? Judging these people harshly. Doesn't the prodigal God, the "wastefully, extravagantly loving God," love them just as much as me?

Curve ball.

Grief, Exile, Welcome

*O Lord, you have enticed me, and I was
enticed; you have overpowered me, and
you have prevailed. I have become a
laughingstock all day long...*
Jeremiah 20:7

It isn't often that Hebrew scripture is the sole text for my sermons, but it is today. I believe the prophet Jeremiah, as a biblical figure to be reckoned with, has much to tell us in today's text. His words are totally relevant to our situation today—politically, culturally, and personally.

Jeremiah was a 6th century B.C. Hebrew prophet. In Hebrew, prophet comes from the word *nabi*, one who speaks for another. A prophet, says Jewish theologian Abraham Hershel, is one who "knew what time it was." Jeremiah knew that the southern kingdom of Israel known as Judah was about to fall, to be lost to the Babylonians. He told the king as much, and the king, as you may imagine, was not happy with that news.

But Jeremiah was right. Judah fell to the Babylonians, and the people lost everything—their home, their known world. And by 587 B.C., the temple itself, the place where the Jews believed that God actually resided, was destroyed. Even the presence of God seemed lost. This experience of loss, of homelessness, of living without certainty, of experiencing the absence of God, was ultimately known as the Exile.

Jeremiah was an exilic prophet. He knew it was coming. He named it. He lamented it. He was angry about it. He was hopeful about the future, but he refused to paper over what had happened. He was not like the false prophets such as Hananiah who abounded at the time and who said, "Not to worry. We will return in just a few years. Things will return to normal in just a short time and we will be back to our former greatness." That was not on the lips of Jeremiah. He named the calamity and its grief and began to live in real hope, even in exile, even in a strange land.

I believe that we are collectively in exile, politically and culturally. It has not been named as such, but we can see it in our political process. This process is just the tip of the iceberg. The real issue, the undercurrent, is the experience of exile. The known world of the 40s, 50s, and early 60s is gone. Fractured and gone. Home as we knew it, whether mythically or realistically, is gone.

Words from my mother in the 50s are the words of that now gone culture. "Carlyle," she said, "be a lady. Be attractive. Marry a doctor, and not just any doctor. Marry a Hopkins doctor." We didn't even need to say that this doctor would be, well, "he," and he would be white and straight. We assumed those attributes because that's what the culture expected.

That world is gone. That homeland has been lost. But some of us long to return to that homeland, to that familiar place where we all knew who had the power, what was expected, who was in and who was out. Our political life plays out this longing.

Exile, loss of home, loss of the known, can also be experienced at the moment the doctor says, "It's cancer," or "It's early Alzheimer's," "It's Parkinson's," or "Your child has leukemia." Or when our partner of twenty-five years says, "I want a divorce." Our known worlds can crumble in a heartbeat. How will we navigate this new place? What can we depend on? And, most deeply, where is God in all of this? *Is* God in this?

Jeremiah, in text and in person, matters in our collective and personal experiences of exile. He shows us the importance of lament. He actually had a hand in writing a book by that name in Hebrew scripture, called *Lamentations*. Lament is so important. Our culture doesn't want us to grieve. When we watch commercials on television, we can see our culture's expectations: be young, be well, be happy. And if you can't be those things, there's a pill that will take care of it.

But lament, grief, is important because it names the real deal. It names exile, the loss of home, the loss of our known worlds. Jeremiah was also unafraid of anger, even anger at God. Because Jeremiah could lament, could give voice to his anger—even at God—he could be solidly hopeful. He was unafraid to engage in a *real* relationship with God, even in a strange land, even in exile.

Jesus is in the prophetic tradition. If you have theological trouble with the Trinity or various forms of Christology that don't make sense, think of Jesus as a true prophet. Jesus thought of himself that way, his mission and ministry formed by the words of the prophet Isaiah. "The spirit of the Lord God is upon me, he has anointed me to bring good news to the poor, to bind up the broken-hearted, to set the captives free, to proclaim the year of the Lord's favor" (Isaiah 61:1). In other words, in whatever exile you experience, there is in that exile the presence of God, just as in today's gospel where Jesus reaches out to lepers—isolated, exilic persons.

This is why church matters in a time of exile, whether it be collective or personal. When church is true church, it speaks the truth. It names the experience of exile, it gives voice to lament, to grief, and to anger. And if it is true church, willing to speak the truth, willing to be in real relationship with God and neighbor, then it can be the locus of hope in the midst of exile.

The ministry of Jesus then and now is to welcome exiles. You and me. My lasting memory of Johns Hopkins Hospital is the huge marble statute in the old lobby—a Jesus with arms outstretched saying, "Come unto me all ye that travail and are heavily laden and I will refresh you."

Transformed

The ultimate result of our relationship with God is our transformation. For some, it comes as a thunderbolt, for others it is a quiet shift toward peace. Transformation is the heart of the spiritual journey. It happens as we are called, awakened, and welcomed.

Heartbreak

"The Longest Night" Service, 2019

WE ARE HERE TONIGHT TO TALK ABOUT, TO OFFER, AND TO SHARE our losses. Loss is an essential part of being human. Each of us has experienced loss, some of us are experiencing loss at this very moment. Loss doesn't have to be experienced immediately to be felt. We know that. We know that we can experience a loss that happened years ago as if it were in this very moment.

We are offering this service tonight because loss is so important, so common, so human, and yet so rarely and honestly shared. Some of us experience our losses most poignantly at this time of year. Everyone is supposed to be happy. The billboards on Route 1 tell us to feel the magic of Christmas, whatever that is. They count the days until Christmas for us and tell us that calories don't count. But those billboards don't talk about loss, about sadness, about grief. So for those of us experiencing loss, loss of any kind, Christmas can feel alien, almost as if it's someone else's experience.

Of course, because our culture does not deal well with loss and grief. We are encouraged to "get over it," to "get on with it," not to talk about it, and to arrive at that mythic place called "closure." We might even say that grief is bad for business during this important commercial season when we are all trying our best to be happy no matter what. But our experience of loss and grief persists. We actually can't "get over it and get on with it" without slicing out a part of ourselves.

Experiencing and talking about our loss and grief is essential. It is exactly what brings us together as human beings. It brings us close because loss is about our true selves, our true humanity. And that humanity is fundamentally about our vulnerability. Try as we might, wish as we might, we cannot control those events, those situations, that bring us grief. We are, as the poet e.e. cummings said, "Human merely beings." Or as the author of the epistle to the Hebrews wrote, we are "beset with weakness." (Hebrews 5:2)

Loss and grief, we know, take many forms.

*the death of a spouse
*the death of a child
*the death of a parent or grandparent
*the death of any close relative or friend
*the death of a vision or an idea
*the death of a pet
*our own deaths
*the loss of a parent, a spouse, or a child to addiction
*the loss of oneself to addiction

*the loss of health, vitality, and physical ability
*the loss of an important relationship

The list is endless.

The actual wonder of our faith tradition as opposed to the Route 1 billboard tradition is that our faith takes loss very, very seriously. In fact, loss in all its forms is at the very heart of our faith. Jesus' own birth, life, and death are stories about poverty, about loss, about grief and suffering not in maudlin or obsessive ways, but reflecting the truth of the human condition. Jesus' first teachings, according to Matthew's gospel, were "Blessed are the poor in spirit, blessed are those who mourn, blessed are those who hunger and thirst for righteousness."

For me, loss was and remains my entry into faith. The daily loss of my father to alcoholism shaped my childhood and opened me to faith, to Jesus, as well as to some core belief that I was not okay as I was. Jesus told me otherwise.

I believe that each of us is here, here in this place, this church, *because* we know loss. For that I am very grateful.

And so, this night I pray that you will ponder and hold your losses, no matter what they are. Know that they are very important to who you are, to whose you are. Know that they are precious and are gifts in their own way, whether recognized as such now or not. Your losses can open you—open you to others, open you to the presence of God. Carry your losses and your grief with you with an open heart.

I want to close with one of my favorite poets, David Whyte, who writes movingly in his book *Consolations* about heartbreak and the consequence of loss. Heartbreak, he says, is both inescapable and inevitable, and is always by our side, not encouraging us to look for another path, but reminding us that it is a foretaste of the final and inevitable relinquishing of all that we have loved.

Ordinary People Transformed

Early on the first day of the week,
while it was still dark, Mary
Magdalene came to the tomb
and saw that the stone had been
removed from the tomb.
John 20:1

THE WONDERFUL THING ABOUT THE BIBLICAL STORY IS THAT it is about people, ordinary people like you and me, and their experience of the presence and action of God within. They are not perfect. Far from it! The biblical story spares no details about the foibles of its characters. They are not one-dimensional. We seem to have made them into paragons of virtue at best or irrelevant at worst. But the truth clearly revealed in the text is that they are ordinary people who are transformed by the extraordinary presence and action of God. My sermon this morning is about three of those people—each one represented in the texts we have just heard. The three of whom I speak are Peter, Paul, and Mary, ordinary people whose encounters with an extraordinary God changed them.

Peter is a real character. He is actually quite lovable because his foibles are so obvious and so like our own. Peter has clear expectations of who God should be and how God should act. Sound familiar? He signs up with Jesus hoping that this will be a way to dump the Roman occupation and bring Israel (and Peter) to glory again. When Jesus mentions that he will suffer and die, Peter is astounded. "Suffer? Die? No way! We need strength and might, not weakness. Not suffering and death." When Jesus takes Peter, James, and John to the Mount of Transfiguration, Peter thinks this is pretty good. "Okay then, this religious experience is okay. Let's just stay here and enjoy it. Don't take me back to that pesky world." I can tell you that sounds very familiar to me. Then, as Jesus' suffering and death draw near, Peter is told that he will deny Jesus three times. "Oh, no, man. Not me. I'm a loyal and faithful guy." But of course, we know what happens when the cock crows three times. Peter is fearful at heart.

I have always found it very reassuring that Jesus said to Peter, "Upon this rock I build my church." Did Jesus have his tongue in his cheek or is this just the truth about those of us gathered at church? We have our definite expectations about who and how God should be. We find dealing with this difficult world daunting, and we would prefer the comfort of a cozy religious experience. We want God to fix things, not suffer among us. And we are often very afraid.

But something happened to Peter. We don't know exactly what. I would call it something like resurrection power.

Something happened to Peter's definite expectations about God and about who qualified to be in God's circle. Some experience of the risen Lord, of resurrection power, changed this man. Deepened him. Opened him. Gave him courage like he'd never had. You can hear it in the Acts text—"I truly understand that God shows no partiality." Or said another way, God's embrace is wide. The experience of the presence of God is for everyone, no matter what. The church has been wrestling with that one sentence, that one statement from the lips of Peter, for years. "I truly understand that God shows no partiality."

Then there's Paul. A real self-acknowledged curmudgeon. Paul was the A-Team's religious person, a Pharisee among Pharisees. No mean feat. He worked hard at keeping the law. He believed with all his heart that the law and keeping it would save him, make him whole, give him life. He was incredibly judgmental of those who didn't or couldn't keep the law, and horrified to hear about this itinerant, country preacher who hung out with all the people Paul would never be caught dead with. People who were everything Paul was not. Flagrant violators of the law! Sinners! This has to stop, Paul thought. He made it his cause to stamp out this nascent movement and get things back on track again. Until one day. Until one day on the road to Damascus, Syria, when Paul was literally struck down by the presence and action of God. Blinded by the light, we might say. Paul could see who he had become—a self-righteous judge. The law had not saved him. It had narrowed him. But he knew deep in his bones that even he, even a self-righteous judge intent on persecuting Jesus' people, could be loved, healed, made whole.

There is probably not a voice in Christendom more powerful on the topic of the power of love than Paul's. Paul knew from the inside, from his experience of the presence and action of God, that the love of God is the power of God, that the love of God is more powerful than the power of death, death in any of its forms. He wrote to the church at Rome, "I am sure that nothing, nothing in all creation will ever separate us from the love of God in Christ Jesus."

And Mary. Mary Magdalene. She is often described as a prostitute, and so misidentified as women often are. We actually don't know much about her other than who she wasn't. She wasn't the "woman of the city" who crashed Simon the Pharisee's dinner party. She wasn't Lazarus and Martha's sister. She was simply Jesus' friend. That is amazing in itself. Jesus meant it when he said, "I no longer call you servants, but friends." Mary was Jesus' friend, a close friend.

When he was hung on a cross, Mary Magdalene was there. She didn't run away. She stayed with her friend. And when they buried him in a tomb, she went to be there too. This was a good and deep friendship that showed its strength not only in life but in suffering and death. She went to the tomb to stay close to this very important friend. And when his body was not there, she was dumbfounded. Where was his body? Then she saw someone near the tomb, and "supposing him to be the gardener," she asked where Jesus' body was. That might be one of the biblical story's best phrases. "Supposing him to be the gardener." The infinite author of all creation incarnate is mistaken as the gardener. How often does God come to us disguised as the gardener?

But when she hears her name called by this supposed gardener, she knows. Hearing is the most intimate of the senses. We all know tons just by how our names are said, whether it's trouble or love. Mary heard love. And she began the telling that lives today.

Peter. Paul. Mary. Ordinary people transformed by the presence and action, the resurrection power of God. The God whose embrace is wide, whose power is love, who calls us each by name.

I pray this day that each of us will be touched and deepened by this resurrection power, so that we can let go of our fears and our judgments and find the presence and action of God in the most ordinary of places—in our own hearts.

Being Human

*Then he began to teach that the Son
of Man must undergo great suffering,
and be rejected by the elders, the chief
priests, and the scribes, and be killed,
and after three days rise again.*
Mark 8:31

FIRST, IT IS ABOUT THE DISCIPLES, THAT CLUELESS GROUP WHO
continually miss the point and who remain clueless to the end.
Actually, I find that heartening. They are not portrayed as saintly,
unctuous, or spiritually mature people They are real.

Jesus talks about suffering and death, and they don't want to
hear about it. This happens not once but twice in Mark's gospel.
"Don't want to hear about that, Jesus. There will be no suffering
and no death."

Anyone who has suffered, and that would be most of us, and
who has tried to tell others about it, knows that it is difficult to
tell and equally difficult for others to hear. Suffering and death
are essential and unavoidable parts of our humanity, but we don't
want to get near them. I get that. As someone I know says, "It's

hard being a human being." A simple and very true statement. The disciples are no different. They are not going there.

Jesus then asks them, "So, what were you talking about on the way?" And sheepishly they answer, "Well... we were talking about who is the greatest among us." Oh, another profound aspect of the human condition—greatness. The drive, the compulsion to be great. Great parents, great students, great artists, great priests, great. The disciples are caught in this trap about greatness, and I think it's directly related to the previous conversation about suffering and death. One way to deny those realities is to focus on being great. It's a strategy. But most importantly, it's part of the human condition.

I get it. I've spent a lifetime trying to be great, and it's costly, it takes a lot of energy, and it results in very little. Plus, it isn't satisfying because we are never great enough! So, we see in this text the utter humanity of the disciples, and I think that is heartening. I hope you can see yourselves in their story too.

But there is also a deeper theme underlying the story of these disciples. A clear core theme is that of incarnation. It is not as clearly laid out as it is in John's gospel, but it is present nonetheless. In fact, it suffuses the text. God *chooses* to become a person, a person who suffers and dies, who experiences vulnerability and weakness, who must let go of all that has been held dear. Not only is it hard to be a human being, it is God's *choice* to take on frail flesh, to meet us precisely in the center of our humanity. Remember that in Hebrew the verb "to love" is the same as the verb "to choose."

Incarnation—embodiment—is at the core of our faith, and it is difficult. Each of us knows that. The gospel texts, the good news, do not shy away from it.

The second theme in this text is death and resurrection. Death because Jesus announces it as part of his humanity, and death in the daily sense because Jesus advocates the practice of daily dying—letting go of our illusions of greatness and becoming least. This is not only a theological theme in Mark's gospel. It is a spiritual practice. Dying to self is dying to that part of us that wants to deny our humanity and wants to be great in order to avoid our humanity. Letting go. Becoming least. Becoming last. Being like the child Jesus places in the midst of the disciples.

That child was the ultimate object lesson for them. Children had no value in their world. Children were far, far from great. But, in Jesus' eyes, they were and are vulnerable human beings. Jesus says to the disciples, "Whoever welcomes (read values, loves, cares for) this child, welcomes me and the one who sent me."

Make no mistake that this is counter cultural and counter to everything you and I have been brought up to value and to be, counter to what our culture pushes and proclaims. The church itself is not immune to the culture's forces.

But the gospel, the good news, presents us with a real human being, Jesus, who was willing to take on all the reality of what that means—suffering and death. And it points the way to the practice for us to follow, to let go, to say the least. Easy? No. Life giving? Yes. Freeing? Absolutely!

Making God Big

And Mary said, "My soul magnifies the Lord."
Luke 1:46.

MOST OF YOU KNOW THAT CAROL DUNCAN WAS A PLANNER. She used planning skills professionally and throughout her life. She chose her place of retirement through careful research and planning. Planning was in Carol's DNA. She planned this service. She chose the readings, the hymns, the Eucharistic prayer. Just about everything in this service was chosen by Carol. So we have to believe that there was clear intention in her choices. While Carol and I did not talk about what her choices intended to convey, it is my homiletical task to discern them. And it's not hard.

Carol intentionally chose the gospel we just heard. This is Mary's song. Most of us hear it on the fourth Sunday in Advent. Sadly, our culture has sentimentalized Mary and made her out to be a placid, one-dimensional, asexual, tame presence. I don't for a minute think that this is what Carol Duncan saw in Mary. I imagine that Carol saw the prophetic, bold, risk-taking woman who proclaimed that her soul, her very essence, proclaimed God's greatness. Luke records her saying, "My soul magnifies the lord and my spirit rejoices in God my savior." In other words, Mary says, "My soul makes God big." Making God big—what a description of Carol Duncan, perhaps even a definition of her calling, her vocation. Carol made God big in her work at the Alexandria Police Department, in her outreach work here at St. Alban's, in her work with the poor, disenfranchised and outcast, both here and in parts of Africa. Carol worked with caregivers for those stricken with HIV/AIDS in Zimbabwe. She even taught them how to quilt! She gave financial support to two Zimbabwean children. She and a friend organized a fundraiser, called Arts for AIDS, for those suffering from AIDS in Zimbabwe. She made God big. Her soul magnified the lord. This is not only Mary's song; it is Carol's song. Carol made God big in her family. Every family has issues, and we have only to look at our own to know that. God never promised us perfection, and Carol did not walk away from the difficulties in her family. She reached out. She gave. She stayed in relationship, and she was generous in all ways. It is one thing to make God big far away. It is quite another to make God big where and with whom we live.

This is Mary's song. And this is Carol's song. My soul magnifies the lord. My soul makes God big.

We know from the gospel accounts that Mary was present at the death of her son. This meant at least two things. First, she risked her own life by being present at the crucifixion because the Roman military routinely killed witnesses. And she had the internal capacity, the presence, the deep love, to be present to death itself. This is never easy, and it is especially difficult in our culture which is so death-denying. Many of us have never been with a dying person or present at a death. Most of us do not want to think about our own deaths or the deaths of those we love. It is probably fair to say that our culture thrives on violence while being in denial about death and dying.

This was not true of Carol Duncan. In my thirty-seven years of ordained ministry, I have never met anyone so intentional, so clear, so planful about her own dying. When Carol got the diagnosis of late-stage pancreatic cancer, she was very clear that she did not want any life-lengthening treatment. She wanted to spend her remaining days sorting out her material possessions and being with her family and friends. And that she did! A little over a month before her death, she gathered those close friends who could come to New Harmony for a two-day retreat at Vicki and David Campbell's home. I told Carol then that I don't even want people around when I have the flu, much less feeling as sick as she did. But gather with her we did. It was part of her plan.

That time in New Harmony is among the most remarkable and memorable of my life. Eight of us sat in Vicki and David's living room for Eucharist, for communion. I asked everyone to tell Carol the one thing they wanted to share with her. When each of us had done that, Carol, who was incredibly weak, proceeded to go around the coffee table sharing what she remembered and loved about each of us. It was one of those holy moments when the divine is so clearly present and palpable. Indeed, it was HOLY communion. The presence of God was made very big in that New Harmony living room. Carol continued to give gifts throughout our two days. Everyone received something that Carol had planned, planned weeks ahead, such as framed pictures and special jewelry.

While I was thinking about this homily, I read a quote from a blog that the rector of St. Alban's, Deborah Meister, posted. It is a quote from the writer May Sarton. It describes Carol Duncan perfectly.

> *I would like to believe that I have given myself away like a tree*
> *that sows seeds every spring and never counts the loss, because*
> *it is not loss, it is adding to future life.*

Carol gave herself away like that tree. We are the privileged recipients of her many gifts, not least of which was the presence of someone who showed us how to die well, and in the process, how to live well.

Now she rests in the arms of a loving savior, in peace with all the saints who have made God big.

To Be Loved

*And now faith, hope and love abide, these
three; and the greatest of these is love.*
1 Corinthians 13:13

Often the scripture we hear on Sunday morning can be incomprehensible. We actually don't know what is being talked about, who the characters are, and in fact, aren't sure why we should care or what these obscure stories have to do with our lives. But we endure, hoping that some meaning will be gleaned from these ancient texts.

On other occasions we hear scripture that we've heard many times before and believe that we understand it. Some passages are so familiar that some of us know them by heart. This morning's epistle is one of those. Most often we hear First Corinthians 13 at weddings. Since we are gathered at weddings to celebrate love, the love between those marrying and our own, it makes perfect sense to hear this part of Paul's letter. However, if we listen closely to Paul's description of love, we may have a second thought or two. "Love is patient; love is kind; love is not envious or boastful or arrogant or rude. It does not insist on its own way; it is not irritable or resentful" (1Corinthians 13:4-7). Well, if I put my own marriage up against Paul's description of love, could I say that I am always patient? Always kind? Never irritable or resentful? I don't think so. If I put Paul's words side by side with my own marriage does it mean I'm not loving?

Is Paul's letter to the church at Corinth just another prop in the cultural adoration of romantic love? Is this portion of Paul's letter another idealized description of the love we are urged to find at all costs in order to be truly happy? Think about it. Our advertising industry is virtually organized around making romantic love happen for us, making us attractive enough, rich enough, healthy enough, virile enough, without pain or blemish. Even the internet has gotten into the game. There is *Match.com* and now *Christian Mingle.*

But most of us are old enough and been married long enough to know just how empty the promise of romantic love can be. Fun while it lasts and delightful, but not the core substance of a lifelong relationship. And, wedding liturgies aside, this portion of Paul's letter to the church in Corinth is not about romantic love. Paul would be horrified to know what we have done with his words.

This portion of Paul's letter is addressed to a church community run amok in his view. Paul has no sooner left after founding this little group than the church in Corinth has divided into factions and begun arguing about which spiritual gift is the greatest and who has it. They have lost sight of the one thing necessary in our lives and in the life of a church community—love. Not romantic love, but God's love. *Agape* in the Greek. Unconditional love. *Aheb* in the Hebrew. Choosing love, knowing love.

Paul had first-hand experience of this love and its transforming power. By his own description he was an arrogant, very religious, practically perfect Pharisee who was working day and night on saving his own soul, when he wasn't trying to do in those pesky followers of that heretic named Jesus of Nazareth. Then one day, an ordinary day on an ordinary journey, Paul was struck dumb. He was literally blinded by the love of God which had nothing to do with how righteous, how perfect, how religious, how zealous he was. He was saved, made whole, loved into new being. He had the good sense to know that this was a love he had not earned, had nothing to do with whether he was good or perfect or right. This love was pure gift, pure grace, out of the blue. For once, he was at a loss for words. He couldn't explain it, although he kept trying as he founded those little communities throughout the Roman world.

This love, this experience of the love of God, is at the heart of all of Paul's letters and explicated most clearly in today's epistle. It is *the* spiritual gift, Paul says. And I would add that this love, God's unconditional love for us, is at the heart of the spiritual journey. It is what you and I seek, and more importantly, it is what seeks us. This love is our true homeland as one author says, and it is the ground of our being as another has said. God's love is the one thing necessary, as Jesus says to Martha in John's gospel.

Church, I believe, exists to help us find this love, or rather be found by it. It's not the only place God can find us, that's for sure! But church can help us, especially when it remembers its true homeland. This year, in Luke's gospel stories, we will hear this theme of God's unconditional love over and over. The prodigal son, the one who screws up but is welcomed with open arms. The woman who crashes Simon the Pharisee's proper dinner party and is welcomed. And many, many more stories. They are meant to help us hear ourselves. We are not perfect, we do sometimes screw up royally, and we are always, always welcomed home.

The Eucharist is a constant reminder, in the best sense of that word. It helps us remember what God is willing to do, how far God is willing to go, to welcome us, each of us, home. To be the very presence by which we are fed, where we can truly abide. Where we can truly make our home. Fortunately, Holy Communion allows us to experience the love of God without words—actually one of the best ways.

The spiritual journey itself is simply about opening to the love of God, letting go of our attempts to be perfect or good or righteous or more spiritual than anyone else. To let us simply be, to allow ourselves to be found, to be welcomed, to be loved for all of who we are.

I was with someone the other day who said about a very sick relative, "I don't pray that she lives or dies. I pray that she knows the presence of God and that she knows that God loves her." I thought, "Yes, yes. Absolutely." This is exactly what I pray for you and for me.

The Real Deal

"The spirit of the lord is upon me, for he has anointed me to preach good news to the poor."
Luke 4:18

PREACHING IS NOT AN EASY TASK—WONDERFUL, BUT NOT EASY. Often dicey. Always complex. How does one communicate something simply that isn't simple in a culture that runs on a thirty-second sound bite attention span on a good day? Perhaps in the digital age, preaching is actually irrelevant. Not to mention that sermons are really not memorable. I don't even remember my own! I've always thought of them as rather like Chinese food—good while they last, but not for long.

In Luke's gospel this morning we hear Jesus' first sermon. We know from last week's continuing story that the feedback was not positive. The people were ready to run Jesus out of town for what he said in His first sermon. You'd think they would have been a little gentler with someone from their own synagogue. And, you'd think they would have been grateful. It was a very short sermon.

He chose the text (Isaiah chapter 61), read it ("The spirit of the lord is upon me, for he has anointed me to preach good news to the poor"), and sat down to preach, as was the custom in synagogue worship in those days. The sermon was one sentence long! Here it is in its entirety—"Today the scripture has been fulfilled in your hearing." Period. End of sentence. End of sermon. There you have it! That's it! The text itself was one the congregation had heard many times, and it was probably even comforting. So why did the congregation get so upset, upset enough to take Jesus to the brow of the hill to throw him over?

Because they didn't like the sermon, even though it was brief enough even for today's extra-short attention spans. But *why* didn't they like it? Because what they heard, was, "I am it!" "I am the real deal." "I am the one you have been waiting and longing for." "I am the anointed one." "I am *maschia – messiah*." Jesus said, "I, the boy you thought you knew, am the embodiment of the Word, the Word made flesh."

The Isaiah 61 text they had heard many times over, perhaps even committed to memory, was now in their faces. It was one thing to hear that one day the poor would hear good news, captives would be released, the blind would see, the oppressed would be free, and those in debt would be forgiven, but now? *Fulfilled now?* Did the congregation really want their lives upended so drastically and dramatically now? Life as they knew it would be forever changed.

The poor would be doing as well as anyone, as we are, they

thought. There would be no more oppressed class to blame for their troubles. Things would no longer be about "them" or be "their" fault. And what about all those freed prisoners? Do we want *them* in our back yards? How safe will we be? And no more debt in this Jubilee year? The bankers in the congregation were getting very nervous. What about our interest income? The congregation was basically saying, "We don't want the real deal. No indeed! Let's get rid of this guy while we can, and be quick about it, before this thing gets out of hand and spreads!"

Isn't this our real difficulty with Jesus? It's not about the intellectual conundrum of how Jesus can be both human and divine. Better to spend years trying to figure this out than deal with the possibility that this person just might be the real deal, challenging us with a radical new reality. Isn't our real difficulty with Jesus about the fact that maybe we too don't want this reality, this freedom, this new life for ourselves and for others?

I mean, if there are, in fact, no "others," how will we feel good about ourselves? If there are no enemies, how can we explain what's wrong with the world? Or, if there is no more debt, how will we have power over others?

Or even in terms of ourselves, if the good news is really preached and I am meant to hear it, what will happen to me? Can I stand to be healed? Really? I've denied myself all my life in terms of what's wrong with me. Can I live as a healed person? If my oppression is lifted, if I am truly as good and as free as anyone else, there will be no more excuses, and, well, to be honest, I've sort of lived my life by saying, "If only...if only I could..." But now I can. Can I live with that? If what has held me captive all these years is vanquished, who will I be?

If the waters of baptism are for real, if we too are marked and anointed forever as Christ's own by that same spirit Jesus referenced in Isaiah's text, then this possibility for transformation has come close to us, touched us. We are given the possibility of living freely, no longer poor, captive, oppressed, or in debt. And we are anointed to share this saving and healing word. This is nothing less than the work and mission of the church—that would be you and me.

Are we ready for this? This much healing? This much transformation? This much mission?

Maybe G.K. Chesterton was right when he said, "Christianity has not been tried and found wanting. It has been found difficult and not tried."

A Very Good Friday

Let the same mind be in you that was in Christ
Jesus, who though he was in the form of God
did not regard equality with God as something
to be exploited, but emptied himself, taking the
form of a slave, being born in human likeness.
And being found in human form, he humbled
himself and became obedient to the point of
death—even death on a cross.
Philippians 5:8

THIS IS THE EPISTLE APPOINTED FOR PALM SUNDAY, THE DAY
that begins Holy Week. It sets the tone for the whole of Holy
Week, and I believe it contains the central action on the cross on
Good Friday. I believe this text also contains not only Jesus' central
action in life and death but also the core action of our spiritual
practice. This portion of scripture from St. Paul's letter to the
church at Philippi assures us that this is indeed a Good Friday,
in fact a Very Good Friday.

"Let the same mind be in you" speaks not about our intel-
lect—our thinking mind—but our heart/mind, the center of our
spiritual knowing. This "mind" is not about doctrine but about

heartfelt knowing through the practice of emptying. "Emptied himself" is Jesus' central action this week, and especially this day. In Greek the word for emptying is *kenosein* or *kenosis*, meaning emptying or letting go, non-clinging. This practice of letting go or self-emptying is the bookend for the first Sunday of Lent when the devil tempts Jesus in the wilderness to hang on, take, become, be safe, be strong, be full. Jesus rejects those temptations and shows us his core spiritual practice of letting go.

And oh, that is a hard one, a very hard one, for us 21st century Americans. Our whole culture is built on having, holding on, retaining, keeping, filling up, more, more, and more. Spiritually, we are encouraged to have the right beliefs and stick to them, keep them, prove them.

What does Jesus let go of? He "did not count equality with God a thing to be grasped." In other words, Jesus did not sit in judgment. He reversed the Garden of Eden action of taking that apple, that knowledge of good and evil that led to judgments. Jesus let go of judgment and embraced the limits, the weakness of being human. He was obedient to the truth of being human—limited, weak, liable to suffering, mortal.

So, on this Good Friday, this holy Friday, I want to ponder with you about letting go, about what letting go looks like in our lives. And while I tell you a few letting-go stories from others' lives, I invite you to consider what you might relinquish in your own life.

Long ago, in the early days of the AIDS pandemic, I used to visit a man dying of the disease. He was in a Roman Catholic hospital, so there was a cross in front of his bed. He was enraged, furious that he had this disease and that he was dying a horrible death in his late 30s. At first, he wouldn't let me visit since, as a priest, I represented the God who was not helping, not fixing, and not curing. Then one day I went to his room and he invited me in, saying, "I get it. I get it. I've been looking at that cross and I know what Jesus knows, that Jesus is suffering with me. That I am known and loved even in this." I said nothing. We both cried. He let go. That was a Good Friday in St. John's Hospital in Santa Monica, California.

Here are some questions to consider.

Is there any anger, resentment, deep disappointment, grief, that we need to let go?

I know a woman who has spent almost half of her life trying to forgive her nephew for contesting his mother's (her sister's) will. She finally came to a place of forgiveness.

Is there anyone we need to forgive? Is there anyone we can release from our judgment?

Bishop Mariann Edgar Budde, bishop of Washington, D.C., told a story recently about a former parishioner, very active and self-giving, who was dying, who was afraid, who was worried that she wasn't good enough, that her life hadn't been as well-lived as she had hoped. Bishop Mariann remembers thinking, "Well, if you're not good enough, we're all in trouble." But that's not what she said to the woman. Instead, she said, "It's okay. There's only love on the other side."

Are there regrets we need to let go of? Are there self-doubts we need to let go of? Can we let go of feeling not good enough?

There are countless thoughts, actions, and beliefs that each of us needs to let go of. This is why self-emptying, *kenosein,* is a life-long practice. This is where the "practice what I preach" comes into stark focus. Letting go, for me, is a life-long, unending process.

But letting go, emptying, is precisely where the extraordinary good news of this day lies. We are given this mind—this mind/heart center—with Jesus. We are not on our own here. This is not another boot-straps practice. We have this mind, this heart-center, that was in Christ Jesus. We can participate in the mind and heart of Christ. We can allow Jesus' heart to beat with ours.

We can know and experience the fruits of letting go, of sharing in this heart/mind center.

We can become more responsive rather than reactive to difficult events in our lives.

We can know that not only is love on the other side, love is here and now.

Letting go, participating in the mind and heart of Christ, is the Way of the Cross and it is the Way of Life.

Epilogue

The Jesus I Know

THERE ARE AS MANY VIEWS OF JESUS AS THERE ARE THOSE WHO have them. I describe in one of the sermons in this book the person who said, "I think God is wonderful. I think the Holy Spirit is lovely. But Jesus—Jesus—I have trouble with Jesus." We should all be having trouble with Jesus, because he is more about practice than belief. And the practice is riddled with potholes.

I grew up in a small town just north of Baltimore. We were outsiders in a "blue blood" part of the city, and I learned early what it was like to be on the edge, watching but not participating. My father was an alcoholic, and as anyone knows who grew up in a similar family, alcohol is the primary relationship for an alcoholic. Again, I was an outsider desperately wanting his attention and having it denied to me.

As a young child, I attended church services with my mother, and I remember reciting the general thanksgiving from the 1928 prayer book. "For all thy goodness and loving kindness to us and to all men." Jesus' presence was very real to me then. As we walked home, I felt that Jesus was walking behind me.

But, with time, going to church began to wane in importance to me. Nevertheless, I never lost the spark to know, to find out, to uncover meaning. By the time I was an adolescent I was reading Spinoza, Durant, Rand, and many others. This intellectual pursuit of religion and philosophy was, I realize now, a way to deal with my sadness about my father.

After graduating from college with a degree in bible studies and religion, I earned an additional degree in the philosophy of religion. Nevertheless, I was not attending church.

At Union Seminary in New York, where I was enrolled in graduate work, a professor said, "Carlyle, you need some experience-based learning." He directed me to a clinical training program at Mass General in Boston. One of the first patients I was directed to was dying of throat and neck cancer. She was very angry and turned to me —twenty-five, immature, scared—and said "Why is this happening to me?"

Of course, I had absolutely no idea, but her question drove me back to church. At 25, I was confirmed at the Church of the Advent, a wonderful place that felt like home.

While at Mass General, I heard the biblical story that has stuck with me and given me Jesus in a way no other story has. It's the story in Luke's gospel about the woman who crashes Simon the Pharisee's dinner party and is accepted and loved by Jesus. This was the story of an outsider whom Jesus sees and loves. I knew then that woman was me. The woman in the story is not attractive and does every embarrassing thing, but she is the very person Jesus embraces. He says, "This woman is forgiven much because she loves much." In that story, I was hearing Jesus. And it was good news indeed.

I found a job teaching religion at a private school outside of Boston, and I also worked part-time at the Episcopal church in town. It was there that I began to put it all together. This was where I belonged. But in 1972, a woman could not put the sentence, "I want to be ordained" in her head, much less say it out loud.

But I wanted to be in a place where the Bible was taught well, since I knew little about it, a place where it was expected that people would worship together daily. So I enrolled at Virginia Seminary, where I was one of three women in a class of seventy. I loved it. I had great professors whom I draw on to this day. And it was there that the Jesus who had been walking behind me as a child began to walk *with* me.

I heard the gospel even more profoundly because I was one of those people—outcasts—who needed to hear it. The text that I had heard years before from Isaiah began to deepen. "The Spirit of the Lord is upon me because he has anointed me to bring good news to the poor. He has sent me to proclaim release to the captives and to let the oppressed go free, to bind up the broken-hearted."

Meanwhile, the political process moving the church toward ordination of women was going full-bore. And it finally happened, in September of 1976, when the vote was cast that changed the canon and would include women ordained to priesthood and episcopate.

I was ordained a priest at All Saints Chapel in Sewanee, Tennessee and became assistant university chaplain at the college. I have never been so clear that it was the right thing, despite the opposition of so many to my ordination. Giving communion to people for the first time as a priest was very moving for me. And while many people would walk out when they saw I was the celebrant, they always stayed when I preached.

Around this time, I began to deal seriously with another outsider issue. Was I a lesbian? I knew that the church would not tolerate that yet, so I kept it a secret but still held on to the Jesus who welcomed outsiders, whose intention was to seek and serve the lost.

I was an ambitious priest and wanted to be a rector. And sure enough, the opportunity appeared. I was called to be the rector of St. Stephen and the Incarnation in Washington, D.C. The church was in one of the most drug-infested areas of the city. I had no experience whatsoever in inner-city ministry and none with drug dealers. But we sat outside with them every evening, and eventually the neighbors began to join us. The choir practiced out there. The dealers became people we engaged, and parents began to feel safe enough for their children to play outside, and our front yard became a kickball court. To this day I believe that what we did there on those evenings was exactly what Jesus would have done.

Nevertheless, I was having serious doubts about my faith and my desire to be a priest.

And then, I developed breast cancer and endured the awful treatment for it. In the midst of that treatment, being sicker than I had ever been, feeling I might die, I heard Jesus say as clear as day, "Carlyle, you have nothing to fear in life or in death." I realized I had been afraid of living. I woke up the next day and wrote down on a legal pad, in rank order, what I wanted to do with my life. Number one was to be in a intimate relationship.

And that's how I met Carol, and we have been together ever since.

I left St. Stephen's and landed in a fabulous parish, St. Alban's, where I stayed for nine years and ended my full-time vocation as their Interim Rector.

While there, I began to learn about and explore the discipline of Centering Prayer. And I began to move into my core spirituality, one that is contemplative. I delved deeper into ancient Christianity's practice, the practice of desert fathers and mothers, the practice of contemporary contemplatives like Thomas Merton and Mother Teresa. It is essentially about self-emptying, what the Greeks call *kenosis*. It is the practice of putting on the mind of Christ, participating in the mind of Christ. Not just learning about Christ, but joining Christ in self-emptying. It is an awareness of there being no separation between God and humans, and no separation between humans and other humans.

My life, especially my suffering and my experiences of being an outsider led me to Jesus. And for the last almost twenty-five years I have been engaged in the discipline of Centering Prayer. Make no mistake—it has not turned me into a sainted wonder. It has also begun to open me to Buddhist insight meditation, which is also about release of self.

The Jesus I am knowing has taught me that we are welcomed in those wide open and spacious arms. That to be ourselves is more than enough.

The Jesus I am knowing has taught me that participation in life, being in life, being incarnate, matters. Sitting on the sidelines is not enough.

The Jesus I am knowing is teaching me that we can all participate in the action and presence of God.

The Jesus I am knowing is teaching me that there is a way to join Jesus in this world and that it matters now more than ever.

The Jesus I am knowing tells me that being human is very difficult and Jesus was willing to become that.

The Jesus I am knowing has not only welcomed me but welcomed countless others, giving me wonderful communities.

For all this, I am profoundly grateful.

Bibliography

Alexander, Eben. *Proof of Heaven*. New York: Simon and Schuster, 2012.

Bourgeault, Cynthia. *The Heart of Centering Prayer: Nondual Christianity in Theory and Practice*. Boulder: Shambhala, 2016.

Bourgeault, Cynthia. *Mystical Hope*. New York: Cowley Publications, 2001.

Bourgeault, Cynthia. *The Wisdom Jesus: Transforming Heart and Mind – A New Perspective on Christ and His Message*. Boston: Shambhala, 2008.

Bruggemann, Walter. *Cadences of Home: Preaching Among Exiles*. Louisville: Westminster John Knox Press, 1997.

Bruggemann, Walter. *The Prophetic Imagination* (second edition). Minneapolis, Fortress Press, 2001.

Buber, Martin. *I and Thou*. Translated by Ronald Gregor Smith. Mansfield Centre CT: Martino Publishing, 2010.

Buechner, Frederick. *The Magnificent Defeat*. New York: Seabury Press, 1968.

Buechner, Frederick. *Peculiar Treasures: A Biblical Who's Who*. San Francisco: HarperSanFrancisco, 1979.

Buechner, Frederick. *Wishful Thinking: A Theological ABC*. New York: Harper-Collins, 1973.

Chödrön, Pema. *When Things Fall Apart*. Boston: Shambhala, 2000.

Dillard, Annie. *Pilgrim at Tinker Creek*. New York: HarperCollins, 1974.

Hammarskjöld, Dag, *Markings*. New York: Alfred A. Knopf, 1964.

Helms, Mary. *Lost and Found*. 2018.

Keating, Thomas. *Invitation to Love: The Way of Christian Contemplation*. New York: Continuum Publishing Company, 2001.

Keating, Thomas. *Open Mind, Open Heart*. New York: Continuum International Publishing Group, 2006.

Laird, Martin. *Into the Silent Land: The Practice of Contemplation*. New York: Oxford University Press, 2006.

Metz, Joannes Baptist. *Poverty of Spirit*. New York: Paulist Press, 1968.

Nepo, Mark. *The Book of Awakening*. San Francisco: Conari Press, 2011.

Oliver, Mary. *Devotions: The Selected Poems of Mary Oliver*. New York: Penguin Press, 2017.

Oliver, Mary. *Evidence*. Boston: Beacon Press, 2009.

Oliver, Mary. *Thirst*. Boston: Beacon Press, 2006.

Rohr, Richard. *Falling Upward: A Spirituality for the Two Halves of Life*. San Francisco: Jossey-Bass, 2011.

Rohr, Richard. *Immortal Diamond: The Search for Our True Self*. San Francisco: Jossey-Bass, 2013.

Rohr, Richard. *The Naked Now*. New York: Crossroad Publishing Company, 2009.

Rohr, Richard. *Things Hidden: Scripture as Spirituality*. Cincinnati: St. Anthony Messenger Press, 2008.

Rohr, Richard. *Universal Christ: How a Forgotten Reality Can Change Everything We See, Hope For, and Believe*. New York: Convergent Books, 2019.

Taylor, Barbara Brown. *An Altar on the World*. New York: HarperCollins, 2009.

Taylor, Barbara Brown. *Bread of Angels*. Boston: Cowley Publications, 1997.

Taylor, Barbara. *Gospel Medicine*. Boston: Cowley Publications, 1995.

Taylor, Barbara Brown. *Home by Another Way*. Boston: Cowley Publications, 1999.

Taylor, Barbara Brown. *Learning to Walk in the Dark*. Boston: HarperCollins, 2014.

Taylor, Barbara Brown. *Mixed Blessings*. Boston: Cowley Publications, 1986.

Taylor, Barbara Brown. *The Preaching Life*. Boston: Cowley Publications, 1993.

Taylor, Barbara Brown. *When God is Silent*. Boston: Cowley Publications, 1998.

The Hymnal 1982, New York: Church Publishing Incorporated, 1982.

Whyte, David. *Consolations: The Solace, Nourishment and Underlying Meaning of Everyday Words*. Langley, Washington: May Rivers Press, 2016.